everyone's a winner!
Over 200 co-operative games and activities for 7-13 year olds

Ruth Wills

Acknowledgements

'Radio Plays' is taken from *Family Fusion*, Paul T. Johnson, SU.

'Birthday cake'; 'Celebrity mix 'n' match'; 'Indian file dodge-ball'; 'Bubbles'; 'Turtle'; '3-legged obstacle course' and 'Musical laps' are taken from *Over 300 games for all occasions*, Patrick Goodland, SU.

'Waxworks'; 'Queenie'; 'Lap ball'; 'Birthday present'; 'Climb the mountain'; 'Partner balances' and 'Spirals' are taken from the web site 'Games just for fun', and these games were developed at the Woodcraft Folk meetings by Mike Cox.

Scripture Union, 207–209 Queensway, Bletchley, MK2 2EB, England.

© Ruth Wills, 2001

ISBN 1 85999 559 4

All rights reserved. The activities in this book may be photocopied for use. This permission is granted freely to owners of this book. This arrangement does not allow the printing of any of the published material in permanent form. Nor does it allow the printing of words or illustrations for resale or for any commercial use. Apart from this, no part of this publication may be reproduced, stored in a retrieval system, or transmitted, in any form or by any means, electronic, mechanical, photocopying, recording or otherwise, without the prior permission of Scripture Union.

The right of Ruth Wills to be identified as author of this work has been asserted by her in accordance with the Copyright, Designs and Patents Act 1988.

Bible text is from the *Good News Bible* published by the Bible Societies/HarperCollins Publishers Ltd., UK © American Bible Society 1992, used with permission. British Library Cataloguing-in-Publication Data
A catalogue record for this book is available from the British Library.

Cover design: PRE design consultants
Internal design: PRE design consultants
DTP: Mac Style Ltd, Scarborough, N. Yorkshire
Illustrations: Pauline Adams

Printed and bound in Great Britain by Creative Print and Design (Wales), Ebbw Vale.

contents

	Dedication	4
	Foreword	5
1	Ice breakers	9
2	Ball games	23
3	Circle games	31
4	Drama games	41
5	Messy games	61
6	Music games	69
7	Parachute games	85
8	Running games	97
9	Team-building games	107
10	Group activities	115
11	Themed activities	139
12	Quizzes	149
	Index of titles	157
	Other resources	159

Key

 Best with 7 or 8-year-olds

 Best with over 11-year-olds

 Lots of space needed

dedication

To all the Wills family.

I would first of all like to thank the Jesson family for all their help and support over recent years. They gave me the inspiration to compile games and activities which are collaborative in nature and, as we have been involved in 'Powerpack' together, I have benefited from our discussions and evaluations. I am also indebted to many people who have given me ideas for this book – thank you to: Susannah Pilkington; David Bartram; Liz Kreeger; Heather Peacock; Heather Bishop; Jenny Boot; Caroline Hammer; Penny Goodchild; Jocella Peck; Phil Brown; David Stokes; Emma Bamford; Alice King; Lizzie Cox; Louise Franks and Derek Goforth.

Finally, thank you to Pam Harrison in Wigan Music Service who taught me 'Obwisanna'; St. Patrick's RC Primary School, Wigan, and Ymgyrch Nefyn Mission, which is where I first began my journey into children's work with SU and where I have learnt many new things.

foreword

Take 20 unchurched children, possibly from broken homes and with varying levels of special needs, at the end of an exhausting school day. Put them in a team, ask them to shoot goals or compete, scoring points against each other, then give the winning team sweets. What is the result? One set of abusive, resentful and hurting children. Does this reflect God's heart for his people? If you have ever been the last to be picked at games, or worried that you may not be picked at all, then perhaps you will understand this.

This scenario is one we strive to avoid in 'Powerpack', the after-school club which we co-ordinate. Powerpack caters for children aged 7–11, mainly from a council estate in Loughborough. Founded on the principle of portraying God's love through all our activities, we feel very strongly that our teaching is reinforced through our programme of singing, crafts, discussion, games and refreshments. Therefore, the idea of introducing collaborative activities came out of our desire to bring God's nature to the children; God's love, faithfulness, peace and care to those whose everyday experiences both at school and in relationships reflect none of these. The result of such an approach is that the children have come some way towards valuing themselves and each other, and also knowing God's love for them regardless of any level of performance.

Key to all of this is relationship: God's relationship with the child; the child's relationship with adults; the child's relationship with other children. Children's work need not be highly skilled in its presentation; what children value is the feeling of being loved and cared for. If through our club we can reveal God's love and care, then we can be the Good News to them. It has been amazing to see the confidence that has grown in these children through simple activities including giving out drinks and biscuits. Everyone is important. Everyone is precious in God's sight.

Psalm 139 says, *'You created every part of me . . . you saw me before I was born'*, and in Psalm 23 we learn that God's *'goodness and love will be with me all of my life.'*

After a day at school, which demands emotional energy, our club provides a framework within which children can relax, learn together, create together and thereby experience wholeness in Christ. We found that they were reluctant to take part in competitive games: they were disruptive and behaved in a self-protective way, so that their failure was not exposed. However, we found that collaborative activities dissolved aggression. They presented an opportunity to experience success all of the time. They built confidence, developed skills, encouraged children to help each other and provided them with an opportunity to receive praise. Children respond to expectation. If the activities we do have the expectation that they will all achieve, they will achieve and will respond positively to our message. Our group's favourite activity is the Spider's web (see page 112), where the children have the opportunity to sit in a circle and just talk and listen to each other. And the wonder that grows as they see the spider's web form in front of their eyes is marvellous to see.

'Let us encourage one another and build each other up . . .' 1 Thessalonians 5:11.

Your children's work may take place in a very different social context to ours. But the ethos can be the same. We are always questioning our approach. Is our message reinforced in our activities? Or do the stories and the games give conflicting messages? Can we preach the message: 'We are all special and Jesus loves us', and then let certain children feel inadequate because their ability to catch a ball is not good enough?

Remember too, that we can learn from the children by listening to them. We are all on a spiritual journey together.

This book provides scope for developing relationships. Alongside a programme of discipline that focuses on positive reinforcement, we saw a marked improvement in our club after a few weeks of collaborative parachute games. But remember that working effectively with children is a long-term process. Keep at it! Our desire is that the activities here will enable you to reflect the nature of Christ in the work you do.

Ruth Wills, Ozzie and Julia Jesson.

NB. You will notice that we have referred to 'children' throughout the book. We do, of course, recognise that 11–13 year olds are not regarded as children but we've simply attempted to avoid repetition of the clumsier phrase 'children and young people'. Please be assured that we mean 'children and young people' throughout.

ice breakers

A couple of years ago, Dave Bartram, then a youth worker in Derbyshire, and I led two lots of club activities for kids aged 11–14. The evening always began with a 'come in' activity or 'ice breaker'. The activities could be done in pairs or small groups and were not advertised as competitions. They usually involved looking at things on the walls; it gave an opportunity for the kids to wander around the venue, interact with others, help each other and see what they could come up with. It was also a great mental exercise for us to think up new ideas! Have a go at devising some of your own. **You can also look in the section titled 'Drama games' for more energetic activities that can be used as ice breakers.**

you will need...
a magazine
scissors
paper
pens
glue

1. Identikit

Collect a selection of current popular magazines. Cut out parts of the faces of several celebrities and stick them all together to make up several amusing new faces; for example, you could have a face made up of Cher's hair; Baby Spice's eyes; Prince Charles' ears; Tim Henman's nose and Dwight Yorke's teeth. Stick the 'new look' faces around the room and, in between these at random, on slips of paper, stick the names of the famous people who have been used. The task is, in groups of as many as you like, to identify and write down which face part belongs to which celebrity.

2. Wordkit

you will need...
paper
pens
scissors

This is a similar game to Identikit, but this time the aim is to make up a story. Write or type out (in a large font) a very well-known story (this may be a Bible story or fairy tale) in very simple terms – approximately five lines would be good. Do this with three or four other stories. Cut up each line of the story into strips and mix the strips up, thereby mixing the stories. Give each strip a number, then stick the strips randomly around the room. The task is to write down which strips go together to make which story and, if possible, to put them in the right order. Share answers at the end.

3. Chart music quiz

you will need...
paper
pens

Preparation: devise a wordsearch which contains the names of several current pop stars. Print this out and photocopy it as many times as you will need (one for each child). Write out the titles of lots of recent chart hits on separate pieces of paper.

Hand out the wordsearch to the children as they come in. Stick onto the walls of the venue the pieces of paper containing the titles of recent chart tracks. The task is to match the names of the tracks with the artists who recorded them. The artists' names are all hidden within the wordsearch.

you will need...
paper
pens

4. Football quiz
Preparation: devise a wordsearch which contains the names of famous football managers. Print this out and photocopy it as many times as you will need (one for each child). Write out the names of as many football clubs as you can think of on separate pieces of paper.

Hand out the wordsearch to the children as they enter. Stick onto the walls of the venue the pieces of paper with the names of football clubs written on them. The task is to match the football club to its manager. The names of the managers can be found hidden in the wordsearch.

you will need...
paper
pens

5. Who are you?
Preparation: devise a wordsearch which contains the names of the members of the group.

After the first evening of your club, or early on in the club's life, collate all the names of the young people on the register into a wordsearch. As they come in at the beginning of the session, ask them to find out each other's names and circle them in the wordsearch.

11

> **tip**
> A warm, friendly, relaxed and safe environment is the best environment to encourage children to acquire skills, learn about themselves and each other, and to build confidence.

you will need...
paper
pens
old calendars
scissors
glue

6. Fred quiz

Preparation: Take an old calendar which has amusing captions and pictures such as those from The Far Side, Dot *or* Fred. *Cut it up, separating the caption from the picture, and stick the captions and pictures randomly around the room. Give each picture a number and each caption a letter.*

The task is for players to match up the picture with the caption, and record the combinations on pieces of paper. This game can be played in pairs or in small groups.

you will need...
paper
pens

7. Where do you live?

If your work is localised and everyone knows the names of the streets in the neighbourhood, try this game.

Preparation: Split up the name of a local street or road into syllables or small parts. Draw pictures to go with each part and stick them around the room.

The task is for players to identify each street from its pictures. For example, in Bolton there is a street named 'Shepherds' Cross Street'. The clue for this would be a picture of a man with lots of sheep and then a cross. You can indicate on the picture if it is a road, street, avenue, drive or whatever.

you will need...
paper
pens

8. Chocolate quiz

Give each person a sheet of paper each with names of chocolate products listed on it. Stick clues describing each chocolate product around the room. The task is to match up the clues with the products. See below for some examples.

1. Birthday, Christmas, New Year etc.
Celebrations
2. Part of the solar system
Milky Way
3. Millions of stars
Galaxy
4. An extra bit of energy
Boost

5. Old American coins
Dime
6. A row of posh houses
Quality Street
7. Flowers sent on Valentine's Day
Roses
8. Wandering musicians in the olden days
Minstrels
9. Something that burns slowly and ends with a bang!
Fuse
10. Eating outside
Picnic
11. Spinning around
Twirl

you will need...
paper
pens

9. Footy fan
This game is the same as the Chocolate quiz, but using the names of football teams instead. Examples are shown below.

1. Great for buns
Chelsea
2. Dracula needs to find a different place to live. He needs a ....
Newcastle
3. The dog keeps trying to escape. You'd better put a .... the gate!
Bolton

you will need...
paper
pens

10. Who's counting?
For this game, the children have the task of filling in the missing numbers and letters in the sentences below. You can make up your own sentences to suit the

age and interests of the children, or base them round a theme, for example, numbers:

3 B _ _ _ M _ _ _.
3 blind mice

_ _ _ days in a l _ _ _ y _ _ _.
366 days in a leap year

B _ _ _ _ _ _ H _ _ _ _ 9_2_0.
Beverly Hills 90210

24 h _ _ _ _ in a d _ _.
24 hours in a day

C _ _ _ _ 22.
Catch 22

Hawaii _ _.
Hawaii 5 0

When I'm _ _.
When I'm 64

1,2, b _ _ _ _ _ my s _ _ _.
1,2, buckle my shoe

52 w _ _ _ _ in a y _ _ _.
52 weeks in a year

you will need...
paper
pens
scissors
card

11. First impressions

This game is to be played when the young people have been together for a short while and are beginning to get to know each other. The aim is to encourage one another and build each other up.

Write or type, in a quite large font, a number of positive qualities that you think are shown in your group, for example, kindness, patience, rapport with children, sense of humour, warmth, understanding. Try to think of qualities that include **all** the young people, including those quieter members or those who don't attend as regularly.

Cut these out into strips, so each word is separate. Also cut out different-coloured squares of card. There should be as many colours as there are people in your group and enough squares so that each player has all the colours.

Lay the strips of paper on the floor or table, face down. One person turns over a strip to reveal a quality. The group then votes by laying down the name of the person who they think reflects that quality. The person who collects the most cards keeps the strip of paper. In this game, each person usually ends up with a strip of paper each, if all the qualities have been chosen carefully! This encourages them to think about each other, not only the people they like the most. The leader can encourage the players in choosing who to vote for, therefore ensuring everyone is given a 'quality'.

you will need...
a ring
a long piece of string

12. Which town?

Preparation: Write the names of various towns on pieces of paper and stick them around the room. Split up the names of these towns into syllables or small parts. Draw pictures to go with each part and stick them around the room too. Label the town names with letters and the pictures with numbers.

The task is for players to identify each town from its pictures and record their answers by writing the number alongside the relevant letter. The town names below will start you off!

Blackpool Luton Mansfield Derby Bangor

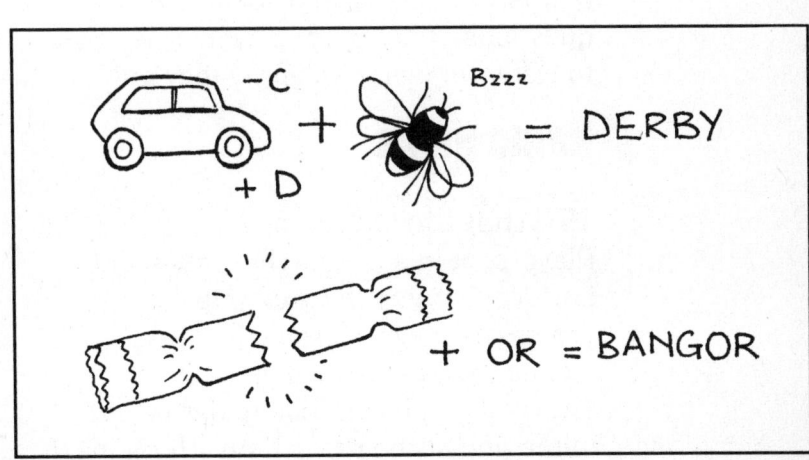

you will need...
paper
pens
black card
scissors

13. Which country?
Preparation: *Draw the rough shapes of countries in the world on black card, so they look like silhouettes. Cut them out and stick them around the room.*
The task is for players to identify the countries and record their answers on paper. To make it slightly easier you might like to put the names of the countries on the wall as well, as in Which town? and ask players to match the shape with the country.

you will need...
sticky labels
pens

14. Celebrity mix 'n' match
Players will have stickers on their foreheads saying the names of celebrities, teams, politicians, and so on. By asking questions of the other players, they have to work out which celebrity they are.

Name games

15. What are you doing?
Players sit in a circle. The leader will perform a mime, for example *cleaning my teeth*. The player to the left will ask: '*Name*: What are you doing?'.
The leader will continue to perform the mime and at the same time tell the next player what to do, for example *combing my hair*.
This continues around the circle until everyone has had a go.
It is actually quite difficult to mime an action and think of another action at the same time – the results can be hilarious!

16. Mexican name wave

The group sit in a circle and say their names out loud one at a time in a clockwise direction. Do this several times, getting faster each time. Each person can also raise their arms as they say their name, just like a Mexican wave. When they have become competent with this, you can then start the wave at two or three points in the circle and even change direction so that some are going one way and others the other. See how far you can keep this going until it becomes total chaos!

> **tip**
> Challenges don't need to be against each other. Challenges against the clock, or against previous group bests, can also work well.

17. In yer face!

This time the group stand in a circle. One designated person leaves their place to cross the circle, in the path of another player. The task is to say that person's name and get into their place. However, the person whose name is called has to leave her place and go to someone else's place. This continues until everyone has had a turn. Then you can speed it up until players are running across the circle and it becomes mayhem, or you can keep it more controlled if you prefer. If any player gets another player's name wrong, then they return to their place and the leader selects another player to begin the cycle again.

you will need...
a flip chart
pen

18. True/False

Everybody is given a list of five questions that they can ask around the group. Questions could be: What is your middle name? Have you ever done any extreme sports? Are you the oldest in your family? Do you play a musical instrument?
Each person is, in answering the questions, allowed to tell one lie. After the questions have been asked, take each person in the group and on flip chart paper record the answers that each person gave, so you can put together an idea of what that person is like, but also try to work out which answer was the lie.

19. Call out

The aim of this game is for people in the group to learn each other's names. The group sits in a circle. The leader says 'go!' and each person can call the name of the person to his or her left out loud at any time. However, if two players call out at the same time, the group has to start all over again. You can vary this by asking players to call out the name of the person opposite them, or the person to their right etc. They will learn more names this way!

20. Introductions

Sit in a circle. Each player takes it in turn to introduce themselves and say something they like to do. With this they must do an appropriate action, for example, 'I'm Ruth and I like to sing.' The next person says their own piece and then repeats what the first person said, for example 'I'm Sharon and I like to knit. She's Ruth and she likes to sing.' And so it goes on around the circle, building up each time.

ball games

21. Dodgeball
Half of the players form a circle with the other half in the middle of the circle. The object of the game is for the outer players to throw a soft ball so that it touches the inner players below the knee only. They dodge the ball if they can! When one is touched, he then joins the outer circle and helps to throw the ball at the people left in the circle. Play until everyone has joined the outer circle, and then swap over.

A variation is **Indian-file dodgeball**, where the inner players are joined in single file at the waist or shoulders and must move together to dodge the ball.

22. Tadpole

Players are split into two groups. One group makes a circle and the other group stands in single file facing the circle (so the shape they make looks like a tadpole – see figure below).

A leader stands in the centre of the circle and throws the ball to each person in the circle one at a time. Each person must throw it straight back. The team counts how many times the ball is thrown. Meanwhile the people in the line run once around the circle, one at a time. When all runners have run around the circle, the people throwing the ball must stop and count how many throws they managed. The teams then swap over. The key to this game is to use a large sponge ball which is easy to catch and to make sure that the players are not spaced too far apart.

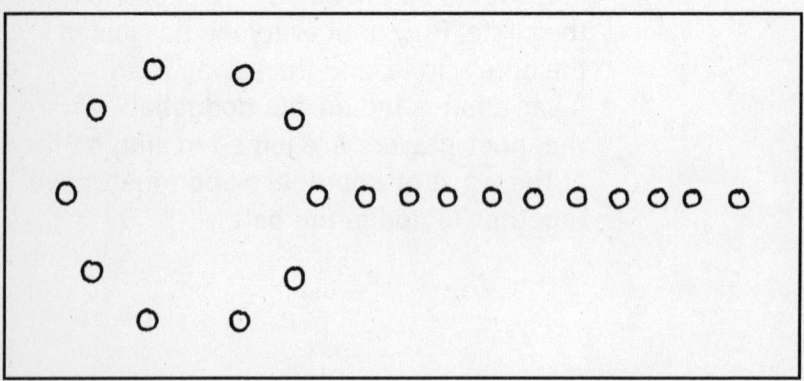

23. Ball madness

The players form a circle with one person (1) in the middle. Player 1 throws the ball to someone in the circle (2) and then runs to swap places with another player (3). Player 3 now has to run into the middle to catch the ball as it returns from player 2 (see figure below). This is a fast-moving game where no one is 'out', but it's fun to see everyone madly running into the middle of the circle.

24. Ball circle
All players stand in a circle. Choose one player to stand in the centre of the circle and one to play from the outside of the circle. The players in the circle face outwards, with their legs apart and feet touching the feet of the people to the left and right of them. The task is for the person outside the circle to bend down and throw the ball through the legs of players in the circle to 'tig' the person in the centre of the circle below the knees. When that player is successful, he can go into the centre of the circle and a new outside player is chosen. Keep playing until everyone has had a turn.

25. Group juggling
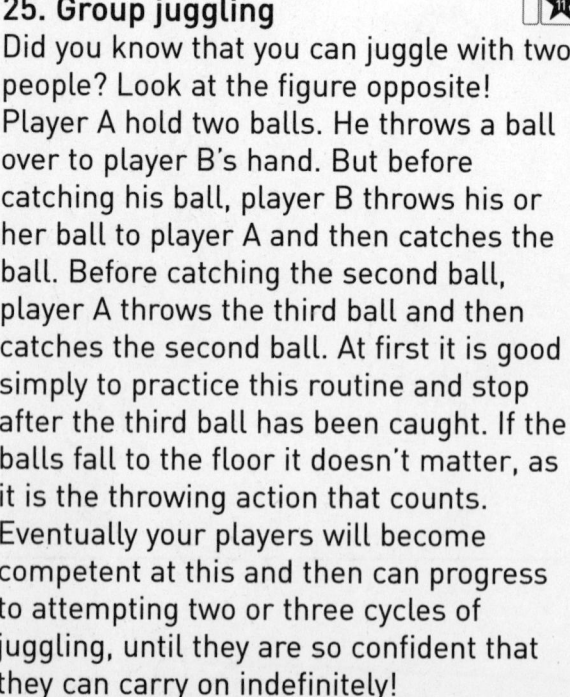
Did you know that you can juggle with two people? Look at the figure opposite! Player A hold two balls. He throws a ball over to player B's hand. But before catching his ball, player B throws his or her ball to player A and then catches the ball. Before catching the second ball, player A throws the third ball and then catches the second ball. At first it is good simply to practice this routine and stop after the third ball has been caught. If the balls fall to the floor it doesn't matter, as it is the throwing action that counts. Eventually your players will become competent at this and then can progress to attempting two or three cycles of juggling, until they are so confident that they can carry on indefinitely!

Juggling can also be done in a larger group. Throw the ball to another player and shout their name as you do so. They then immediately pass the ball on to another player, who does the same, until everyone has had a go. Then introduce two balls and eventually three. It soon becomes very confusing! This game is good for hand–eye co-ordination and for developing skills of concentration and awareness of others. It also encourages listening skills. It can be used as a good name game or ice breaker when your group is new.

> Start new games frequently! The maximum length of time for any game should be 10 minutes, but aim to change games every 4 or 5 minutes. Keep momentum throughout your session!

26. Lap ball

The group sits in a straight line on the floor, close together with their legs touching. A ball is thrown onto the top player's lap and the group must pass the ball down the line without using their hands, only their legs and feet. A more difficult variation is for each person to be on all fours and for the ball to pass from back to back.

27. Queenie

Select a player to become the Queen. She faces a wall and the other players stand behind her without moving. The Queen throws the ball over her head to the players behind. If the ball is caught, the catcher becomes the Queen – but usually there is a mad scramble to get the ball, so nobody catches it! The ball is recovered and secretly hidden behind the back of one of the players. When they are ready, the group chant: 'Queenie O, Queenie O, who's got the ball?' The Queen then turns round and has to guess who has the ball.

28. Hand ball

Split your players into two groups. Each group can give itself a name and devise a chant or shout, to encourage team bonding! The leader throws a ball to the players. The player who catches the ball then throws it to a member of his team, and the team must try to keep the ball with that team. No player is allowed to run with the ball and there is no goal-scoring: it is just a game of catch. For affirmation, each time the ball is caught, that team shouts its chant.

> **tip**
>
> When playing ball games, assess the motor skills of your children before selecting your ball. If the ball is too small, the children may not catch it very often and therefore feelings of failure may creep in. Good balls for older children to use outside are netballs as they are large and heavy, but for games with younger children you could use inflatable beach balls or large sponge balls. There are also many 'fun' balls available in the shops which may be appropriate.

circle games

29. Train-spotting
One player is chosen as the train-spotter and goes out of the room. Four players are chosen as stations. The group stands in a circle and holds hands. The train-spotter comes back in and stands in the middle of the circle. A hand-squeeze (*train*) is passed at various speeds around the circle and the train-spotter has to identify where the train is. When the train enters a station, that person makes the sound of a steam train and can choose whether to change the direction of the squeeze. When the train has been spotted, a new train-spotter is selected, until everyone has had a go.

you will need...
a ring
a long piece of string

30. Ring on a string (variation of Train-spotting)
One player (the treasure hunter) leaves the room. The group stands in a circle, each holding part of a large loop of string which has a ring threaded on to it. The treasure hunter returns and stands in the

31

centre of the circle. The group secretly passes the ring in their clenched fists to each other, and may change direction at any time. The treasure hunter has to identify the location of the ring.

31. Musical laps
Everyone stands in a long line holding on to each other's waists and then forms a circle by the back of the line joining the front. When music is played, the group walks round in a circle. When the music stops, everyone sits down, on each other's knees. If the whole group sits, they are successful. If the whole group doesn't then the circle will collapse so the group may have to try this a few times until they get it right!

32. Fruit salad
The group sits in a circle on chairs or on the floor and each person is given the name of a fruit, for example peach, pear, apple, grape, peach, pear, apple, grape etc. Choose one player to sit in the centre of the circle and one person to be the caller. When *apple* is called, all the people named *apple* swap places with each other. Meanwhile the person in the middle of the circle must try to find a place in the circle. He runs to a spare seat or place, leaving one remaining person who then takes centre stage.

You can call each fruit name individually or, to make the game more lively, call two fruit names at a time, or, to make

everyone change places, shout *'fruit salad!'*
Play until everyone has been in the middle.

33. Props

you will need...
several household items

Select several household items, such as a colander, cheese grater, cricket bat. Around the circle players have to think of an alternative use for each item and mime with it. The cricket bat could also become a large comb or toothbrush, a guitar or a spade, for instance. You can pass the prop around the circle as many times as there are ideas, but any player can pass if he has an imagination block. The game is funny, but don't put any pressure on reluctant players to have a go.

34. 1–10

The group sits in a circle and the leader starts the counting with '1.' Group members must then say the next numbers, in turn, until 10 is reached. The calling will be completely random and the aim is to call a number without calling at the same time as another player. If two do coincide, start again! This requires concentration, awareness of the group dynamic and also some luck!

35. Shoe swap shop

Each player takes one shoe off and puts it on the floor with the other shoes. A circle is formed around the shoes by holding hands. The group must manoeuvre the circle so as to deliver the shoes back to the rightful owners' feet without breaking hands in the circle.

you will need...
a cup
water

36. Water challenge
The group makes a circle and can stand or sit. A cup filled with water is to be passed around the circle, but without using hands! The challenge is for players to keep as much water in the cup as possible while passing it round.

37. Bear in the cage
Choose one player to be the bear. The rest of the players form a circle round him. The bear in the middle of the cage (circle) wants to get out. The players in the circle have to prevent the bear from escaping by working together with their bodies. When the bear does escape, choose another one until everyone has had a go.

38. Magic microphone
The magic microphone can be anything from a plastic microphone to a chunky marker pen. The magic microphone concept is brilliant for group discussions and for allowing every child the opportunity to say something. The only person allowed to speak is the person holding the magic microphone.
Ask the children a question, for example *What is your favourite chocolate*? Then pass the microphone around the circle. Each child answers in turn, pretending to

speak into the microphone. The questions can become more pertinent and personal with questions such as: *What are you afraid of?* This allows children the opportunity to open up. But remember that each child also has the opportunity to pass if they don't want to share. There should be no pressure on them to speak if they don't want to.

39. Crocodile letters
The group sits in a circle. The leader thinks of a word, for example *sausage.* The person to the left of the leader then says a word which begins with the last letter of that word. So, for example, you could end up with a chain such as:
sausage egg goat telephone.
If the group want to set themselves a challenge, they can time how long it takes them to get around the circle each time.

40. Celebrity crocodile letters
The game is played as above, but by thinking of celebrity names instead of nouns: for example ***Desmond Lynam; Margaret Thatcher; Ronan Keating; Gary Barlow.*** However, when the first and last names begin with the same letter (for example Gary Glitter, Roland Rat), then the direction of play reverses.

41. Cookie jar
Start a repeating rhythm: slap knees; clap hands; click left; click right. In time to the rhythm, chant the following verse

using names from the group. Continue until each person has had a go. If the chanting goes out of time, or someone can't think of a name, then stop and start again. Time how long the group is able to keep it going each time.

Chant:
Group: Well Ruth stole the cookie from the cookie jar!
Ruth: Who me?
Group: Yes you!
Ruth: Couldn't have been!
Group: Then who?
Ruth: Well Jane stole the cookie from the cookie jar!
Jane: Who me?
Group: Yes you!
Jane: Couldn't have been!
Group: Then who?

Jane now chooses someone and says that name in the chant

you will need...
items brought in by players from home
a tray
a cloth

42. Are you listening?
Each player brings an object in from home; something that is of special value to them. They sit in a circle with all the objects on a tray in the middle of the circle. One by one everyone in the circle discusses their items. Then each object in turn is covered up by a sheet of fabric or taken away. Players have to remember what toy or item is missing and why it was special to its owner. You can use the magic microphone (see game 38) for this game; this is a

listening game and helps the children to value what the other children say.

you will need...
a bunch of keys
a blindfold

43. The bear and the honey pot

One child is the bear, in the centre of the circle guarding the honey (bunch of keys, placed behind him) and is blindfolded. Another child quietly creeps towards the bear and tries to steal the keys and get back to her place before the bear hears her moving and points at her. If the bear catches the thief, the bear stays in the middle. If the honey is stolen, the thief becomes the bear.

tip

Speed is important; don't mess around with long descriptions or chat – go straight into the game and let players pick it up by a demonstration.

44. The animal game

Players sit in a circle. Each player takes on the character of an animal by making a sound and action for that animal. Before play begins, go around the circle, each player performing their action and naming their animal. The elephant is always the last animal in the circle.

To play, players perform their own action followed by the action of any other player. For example, the player who is the lion performs the lion action, followed immediately by someone else's action, eg the bear. The bear then performs their action followed by, for example, the dog. The play continues: lion/bear/bear/dog/dog/mouse, etc until a player forgets or makes a mistake.

That player then becomes the elephant and sits in the elephant's seat. All the players then move along one place, until the empty place is filled, each therefore taking on a new animal. No one is ever out in this game, so play until it gets boring and then choose a livelier game!

45. Music man

Send one player out of the room. While they are away, select one player to be the music man. All the other players will be the 'band' and will follow his or her actions. When the first player re-enters the room, the 'band' will play by imitating the sound and action of an instrument, for example drums, violin, trumpet, etc. The leader then changes instrument and the rest of the 'band' follow. The first player must work out who the music man is.

46. Knees pile up

All players sit on chairs in a large circle. The leader of the game shouts out things like, 'if you are the eldest in your family, move one place to the right.' The players who are the eldest in their family then move one place to their right. If there is a free chair, then they sit on it. But if someone is already sitting on the seat, then they have to sit on that player's knee. This continues as the game progresses, and so players pile up on each other's knees. Players can only move to respond to a statement if they are on the top of the pile! The game ends when the first player has returned to his or her seat. The game is completely random with no winner or loser; just a good laugh!

drama games

The purpose of drama games is, as well as developing performance skills, to break down barriers between people, reduce inhibitions and build up confidence. The games are mainly intended to allow for self-expression and have positive outcomes. They also sometimes allow the players to go a bit crazy! Most importantly, there are no rights or wrongs. They are fun and encourage team-building as well as individual skills. I always begin with a brief warm-up to relax and stretch muscles.

47. Warm up
Stretch each arm up into the air, one at a time, out from the waist and as high as possible. Stretch out even the fingers. Then flop, the body relaxing and hands hanging towards the ground. Circle the shoulders round, first to the front and then to the back. Shrug shoulders and then lower them. This helps to loosen up tense bodies. Let the head fall to the chest, by relaxing the neck. Then circle the neck round to the left and to the right. Do this several times. Finally, let the head flop from side to side, ears reaching to the shoulders (without moving the shoulders up to meet them!).

48. Vocal games

It is also important to warm up the voice before any acting, as the voice is the most important instrument we have and needs taking care of. Try any of the following.

Preparation: Vocal games make use of **diaphragmatic breathing** which can be assisted by lying with the back on the floor and placing a book on the stomach. (The diaphragm is the stomach muscle, and good sound control comes from here, not the chest.)

Breathe in through the nose, and out through the mouth.
Diaphragmatic breathing should move the book up and down. When standing up, place hands on stomach and breathe in. The diaphragm muscles should push the hands out. When breathing out, the hands should come back close to the body.

Some exercises to try:
- Breathe in *through the nose* and hold your breath. Hold your finger in front of you as if it were a candle. Gently breathe out and pretend to make the candle flame flicker. Now breathe in again and this time breathe out more quickly so the candle flame is blown out. Finally, imagine there is a cake full of candles to blow out: blow them all out with a big blow from the stomach.
- Breathe out through the mouth and 'sigh' each vowel sound with a slight 'h'

at the beginning, for example hayyyyyyyyyy heeeeeeeeeee hiiiiiiiiiiiiiiiiii hoooooooooo huuuuuuuuu.
- Try breathing out and repeating the vowels aeiou until you have only a little breath left. Breathe out the remaining air.
- Increase the volume of each vowel sound as you breathe out by increasing the speed at which the air leaves your diaphragm.
- Now imagine you are blowing out a single candle or many candles and give louder shouts. This is good breath control.

49. Magic gobstopper

Imagine that in your mouth you have a magic gobstopper. Rather than getting smaller as you chew it, it gets bigger! Begin to chew as it is small and requires small movements. As it grows, move your face muscles more and keep on exaggerating the movement until it becomes bigger than your mouth! Use your eyes and all of your face muscles to keep you relaxed and feeling alive.

50. Escaping noise

Imagine that there is a noise inside your body which is trying to escape. Imagine it starting in your stomach, and then rising up through your chest and to your head. As you do, breathe in through your nose, using diaphragmatic breathing. When it is ready it will escape, so shout the noise as loudly as you can, in your own time.

51. I am not guilty
Players sit in a circle and, beginning with a whisper, one by one say 'I am not guilty.' Each person in turn should speak slightly louder than the one before. This takes good breath control and concentration in order to increase the sound carefully and not to shout or strain the voice when getting louder. When you feel the loudest volume has been reached, progressively lower the volume until a whisper is again reached.

52. AEIOU
The group stands opposite the leader and repeats the vowels *aeiou* over and over. The dynamics are determined by the leader: when he walks forward the sound should get quieter, and when he walks back the sound should get louder. Again, this requires good breath control.

53. Sound picture
In the group, the idea is to build up a collection of sounds to recreate a scene. For example, to recreate an office, there could be the tapping of a computer keyboard, the whirring of a photocopier, the ringing of a phone, the whistling of a kettle and the chattering of voices. The sounds are made using the voice or body, and each person joins in one at a time, building up the picture until the whole group is performing together. A variation of this activity could be to send one player out of the room and for them to come

back in and guess the scene that is being imitated.

Mime games

Obviously, there is no vocal preparation needed for mime games, but they are excellent for improving communication skills within the group and encouraging awareness of how we relate to each other in non-verbal ways.

54. Chinese actions
This game is a variation on Chinese whispers, to be played by five people. Choose three players to leave the room (1,2,3) and two players to stay (4,5). Player 5 performs an action to player 4, eg cleaning windows or baking a cake. Player 3 then enters the room and player 4 performs the same action to him. Player 3 then performs the action to player 2, player 2 to player 1 and finally player 1 must guess what player 2 is miming. As in Chinese whispers, a lot will have changed as the mime moves from player to player and it becomes hilarious for the audience, or the other players watching!

55. What's my line?
Select a player to stand in the middle of the circle. This player chooses a mime which he then performs. It could be, for example, baking a cake or gardening. The other players in the circle then have to try

to work out what he has been doing, and when one player thinks they have worked it out, they can then step into the middle of the circle and take over. As more players think they know, they also take over from the player in the middle until everyone has had a go. At the end of the game, everyone says what they were doing to see if they were right. This game is like a mimed Chinese Whispers.

tip

Change the game every three or four minutes. The drama session should be fast-moving and interactive at all times.

56. Eye contact

Members of the group walk around the room in time to a beat from a tambour. Each person walks in their own path and space. No one is to make eye contact with anyone else, so there is no relationship between individuals. Then stop and rest. During the rest time, ask the players how they felt doing this. They may have felt alone, isolated, distant or nervous. It also may have been a positive experience of solitude. There is no correct answer, but it will be interesting to hear their responses. Now do the same thing again, with people walking in their own space, but this time making eye contact. Again, ask how they felt. What have they learnt about eye contact and relationships? As an extension, split the group in half, and repeat the activity with one half of the group observing the other half. Ask each group what they observed.

57. Ice melt
Group members walk around the room in time to a rapid tambour beat. When the tambour is banged loudly, they freeze in position. Then slowly, and in their own time, they pretend to melt, beginning with their fingertips and then leading up their arms into their torso and legs, until they are lying on the floor. The opposite can also be done. From the tambour bang, slowly grow up, beginning with fingertips, to an interesting pose, and freeze. This activity encourages whole body movement in drama, increases spatial awareness and self-expression.

58. Body language
The group members walk around the room, again in time to a tambour beat. The caller then bangs loudly on the tambour and the group freezes for 10 seconds. The caller shouts out an adverb (for example, angrily, happily, miserably, mischievously) which will determine the manner in which the group should then move. They must use the 10 seconds to think of a situation where they have previously experienced such emotion or action. The memory should enable them to take on the emotion in order to move in that way. Body language and facial expressions will convey the emotion.

As an extension, one player could leave the room and when he returns, should try to guess the adverbs which the other players have chosen for themselves and which they are now expressing.

59. Mirrors
In pairs, players stand opposite each other and take it in turns to be the leader. The leader makes shapes and patterns with his body, and the other player has to produce a mirror image of his movements as quickly and accurately as possible. This focuses on concentration skills.

60. Picture postcard
This activity is similar to game 53: Sound picture.
Suggest a scene for a picture: a beach; a Christmas party; a railway station. Each person in the group takes it in turn to adopt a pose from the given scene in order to build up a picture. For example, in a railway station, one player may stand, looking at his watch, with a sad face, as if he had missed a train. Next to him might be a guard, blowing his whistle for the next train. When each player is involved, the whole group freezes and the picture postcard is formed. This gives a good opportunity to explore facial expressions and body language.

61. Photo story

This activity can be done in small groups. Each group is given a popular story title and must prepare four static scenes from the story by adopting suitable poses and freezing in a tableau. When presenting to the group, the audience can close their eyes in between 'shots' so that the illusion of the photo story is kept. Facial expressions are vital here to convey the emotions of the characters in the absence of speech.

Silly games

These silly games can be used as ice breakers at the beginning of your club, and they are also great for having a good laugh with a non-competitive focus.

62. Say what you mean!
In this game, the leader calls out an action and everyone must do the opposite. Therefore, if he says 'stand up', then everyone must sit down. When mistakes are made, carry on with the game because no one is 'out'.

63. 'If you love me honey, smile'
One player is selected. He chooses another player, sits on her lap and says, 'If you love me honey, smile.' The other player then has to respond by saying, 'I do love you honey, but I just can't smile.' This must be done without smiling, laughing or giggling! If a player laughs, he or she is then 'on' and sits on the knee of any random player to continue the game. If no one is laughing, the player who is 'on' originally moves from player to player until he does make someone laugh.

64. Jump in
Members of the group stand in a circle. They are all given a style, for example a Blue Peter presenter or an American president, and the name of a fruit, such as a banana. When the leader calls out 'JUMP!' players jump into the circle,

shouting the name of the fruit in the style they have been given. This can be played individually, in small groups or by the whole group at the same time.

65. Horsemen, knights and cavaliers

Players find a partner and the pairs move around the room to music. When the music stops, the caller shouts out the following instructions to be followed:
Horsemen: one of the pair scrambles down on all fours like a horse and the other one sits on him.
Knights: one player goes down on one knee and the other sits on his spare knee.
Cavaliers: One jumps into the other's arms.

66. Blob

Players sit in a circle. They are to imagine that a big squashy blob has come down from outer space and landed on the face of one of the players. He shows this by covering his face. Also, some of the blob has splatted onto the players to the left and right of this player, so they put their hand onto the cheek which is closest to the 'blobbed' player. This player then, using sound effects and as much drama as he can, has to mime removing the blob from his face and passing it on to another player, by throwing his hands in their direction. The play continues across the circle and around the group until everyone has caught the blob, or the group begins to get bored. It is a hilarious game and a wonderful opportunity for more eccentric and confident group members to express themselves!

> **tip**
>
> In silly games, everyone needs to be embarrassed, not just one or two players. The whole group can then feel as though they have had the same experiences and no one is singled out. If players are not happy making a fool of themselves, then stop the game and do something else.

Any of the circle games can also be used as ice breakers in drama workshops.

Team activities

you will need...
boxes of a variety of sizes and shapes
a random selection of props and costumes

67. The wall game

This was a TV programme when I was a young teenager. I loved it!

Take any number of cardboard boxes of varying sizes and shapes. The boxes are to form the set for a quick sketch. In groups, each team is given the title of a sketch, and has 15 minutes in which to create the set, write and rehearse the sketch. Each group then performs the sketch. The subjects of the sketches can be anything from current affairs issues to retelling stories or role-play.

> **tip**
>
> Drama sessions enable inhibitions to be broken down. You can use any of these activities as ice breakers at the beginning of your teaching sessions.

> **tip**
>
> An ancient proverb says:
> 'I hear, I forget,
> I see, I remember,
> I do, I understand.'

68. Instant drama

This is a good time-filler, but can also be used as a way into Bible teaching. Don't forget that children remember more of what they *do* than what they *see* or *hear*. Take a popular Bible story, for example, the Lost Son, the Good Samaritan, etc. Read it aloud from the Good News Bible or CEV. As the characters are introduced, select people from your audience to play these characters and, as you read, they mime along to the story. This can be hilarious, especially the pigs scene in the Lost Son! Because this game is unrehearsed, it is spontaneous and fresh.

69. Adverts

Using the props, the group has to write an advert to advertise that prop. However, they should think of an alternative use for the prop; for example, the juggling club could become a milk bottle.

70. Machine

In groups, the players must use their bodies and voices to create a moving machine (see illustration). The machine must have a purpose and must work! It may even transport an object. This activity is good for discussion and co-operation amongst players.

you will need...
a random selection of props, which can be incorporated into the drama

71. Bible stories with a difference
Each group is given the task of retelling a Bible story 'in the style of', for example, a scene in a Spaghetti Western/Star Trek/Star Wars/a period drama. A very important tip is to read the passage in the Bible several times for details and accuracy in the story. If it is a gospel account, read the story in the other gospels too. Don't weaken the story, add or take away anything.

72. Modern storytelling
You could also try retelling a Bible story in a modern setting, making sure to use props, for example, a tea cosy or a juggling club.
One group of teenagers on a church weekend decided to tell the story of the three servants with the talents, as found in Matthew 24. However, the master was the Prime Minister who commanded his politicians to look after the country while

he went on a foreign tour. They were left with the task of recruiting more members to the party. The first politician went out on an open-top bus with his megaphone and recruited a thousand more members. The second politician went knocking on doors and recruited two thousand more members. The third and lazy politician sat at home and played on his PlayStation and recruited no members. Well, you can imagine what happened when the Prime Minister came back...

This method of using drama is great for enabling the players to think about what the story really means and what message Jesus is conveying, as well as producing an exciting play.

Role play

Role play enables your group to engage with characters and become a part of situations in the Bible context. They should relate to the characters and situations and learn from them by being a part of them. I suggest that before any role play activity begins, you give your group plenty of time for research. This may involve reading several versions of the Bible story, reading a study Bible, or even watching video footage from films such as *Jesus of Nazareth*. It is also good for them to think about contemporary situations that parallel the Biblical one. This promotes empathy for the characters they are to portray. As preparation, you could play one of the games listed below:

- Split the children into pairs or threes. Give them an object, and then ask them to improvise a scene which uses that object.
- Ask them to improvise an advert for the object you have given them.
- Ask them to make up a story, by going around the group, with each player adding a line at a time. You can add interest by giving them objects, people, places or words that must be incorporated into the story.
- Give the players a scenario that they must improvise in pairs or small groups, for example, 'the park bench', 'I've got a secret,' or 'what are you doing?'
- Ask the players to change the way they are acting, so that they act 'in the style of' (as above): for example, 'in the style of' a children's TV presenter.
- Ask the players to improvise a scene, for example mowing the lawn and, halfway through, shout 'freeze!' They do so, then replacement actors come on to take over and continue the scene, perhaps in a completely different way. For example, they might turn the lawn-mowing action into rowing a boat.

73. TV report

One group member is a reporter commenting on the scene of an incident. In the background, other players are acting or miming the scene, and can be interviewed during the course of the report. Scenes could be, for example: the feeding of the five thousand, the call of the disciples, the wedding at Cana, the healing of the paralysed man, or the Resurrection.

74. Press conference

Choose three or four players to sit behind a press conference table, and let the others be reporters. Choose a scene from the Bible (a good one is the raising of Lazarus in John), and allow your players time to research the situation first, by reading the Bible account. The reporters should then write down some appropriate questions, and the others should think about their answers to the questions. Players can sit behind a table and reporters sit on chairs in front of the table. Make sure that there is a leader who can control the proceedings and take on the character of a master of ceremonies to keep things moving. The reporters ask their questions and the answers are given by the Bible characters.

75. Character empathy

Imagine you are a Biblical character after a significant event; for example, Peter after he had denied Jesus, Moses after the burning bush, or Pilate at the time of the trial.

Think about the main issue in the story. In the story about Peter, it is letting down a best friend. In preparation, ask the player to think of a time when he has been let down, or has let someone else down. The player can write about the situation and feelings involved, or share them with a partner or small group. After spending time looking at the text and the passages leading up to the incident, allow the player to improvise a short scene relaying how he feels about what has just happened.

I tried this activity with a group of theological students in Croatia. The effect was profound. After listening to 'Peter' tell how he had denied Jesus, we were all deeply moved and realised that we also have let Jesus down. What followed was a time of prayer and repentance for the things we had done wrong. The drama had communicated our need for forgiveness in a very real way.

Below is a near representation of what was improvised.

Peter and the denial

Disciples are sitting by the fire, warming their hands. Peter walks on, looking sad.

Disciple 1 (*to the rest*): Here comes Peter, everybody. Look at him, he looks as if the world is going to end! Oi, Peter! What's up? What's the matter?

Peter: No, please Andrew, I want to be on my own. *Starts to walk away.*

Disciple 1: Come on, it can't be all that bad. Tell us, why are you so sad? We can help!

Peter: No one can help now. I've gone too far and this time I have to suffer the consequences.

Disciple 1: But what can be so bad? Sit down with us, Peter, and tell us.

Peter sits and joins the others.

Peter: It's Jesus. Well, not Jesus, me. Well what it is, is ... (*buries his head in hands*) I denied Him! He is my best friend. I am his loyal follower and I have let Him down! I told Him that I would be willing to die for Him, and now I have done this!

Disciple 1 (*quietly*): Oh. Tell us what happened.

Peter: After we had all been in the garden with Jesus and I had that fight with the High Priest's slave ... well, Matthew and I went and followed Jesus to the courtyard of the High Priest's house. Jesus went inside. I stayed outside in the yard. While I was waiting, a girl saw me and asked me if I was a disciple of Jesus. Well of course, I should have said yes ... but I didn't. It was as if fear had gripped me and suddenly I was ashamed of following Jesus. 'No, I am not,' I said to her. And then, later, as if I had not done enough

damage, when I was warming my hands by the fire, other people asked me the same question: 'Are you one of the disciples of that man?' And again, I replied, 'No I am not!' As I said that, the cock crowed three times, just as Jesus said it would.
Disciple 1: 'Before the cock crows three times, you will say that you do not know me.' That's what Jesus said to you, I remember. But what happens now, Peter?
Peter: Jesus has been taken before Pilate, to be tried. He may die. I'm afraid. I'm devastated. What shall I do?
Peter walks slowly off-stage with his head bowed.

> **tip**
>
> In improvisation, when you are imagining that you are another character, cast your mind back to a similar experience from your life, and remember the feelings you had then, and what you did. Then transfer those feelings to the character you are playing. The drama will become very real to you, and you will have more empathy for the character you are playing.

messy games

you will need...
spaghetti
a bowl
a fork

76. Spaghetti quiz
Preparation: cook the spaghetti; everyone must wash their hands.
This game is a group quiz where you can play against the clock, or you can play the game several times and try to improve the performance of the group each time. Ask the group questions about the teaching or theme you have been covering. Take a piece of spaghetti. Each person who answers a question correctly takes a piece of spaghetti and ties it to your piece of spaghetti. Keep on going, tying pieces of spaghetti together until you have run out of time, or until the spaghetti string breaks.

you will need...
several tins of alphabetti spaghetti
spoons
plastic plates
bowls

77. Alphabetti spaghetti
Preparation: tip the contents of each tin of spaghetti into a bowl; everyone washes their hands.
The task is to make words using the spaghetti letters. The words can be either a poem players have learnt, or the names

of every group member. Move the letters using the spoons, and make sure that players wash their hands before and after playing this game!

78. Eclair memory verse

you will need...
chocolate eclairs
piping icing in tubes
plates
a knife

This is a fun way of learning a verse. Give each child a chocolate eclair and a word or words. It is their task to write the word(s) on their eclair using icing. Once everyone has completed the task, ask them to line up in the correct order, holding up their eclair, to form the verse they have learned. One by one, the children can eat their eclairs, but each time an eclair is eaten the verse must be recited. Eventually all the eclairs will be gone but the children should be able to say the verse off by heart.

79. Messy morning

I will always be grateful to Ymgyrch Nefyn Mission (SU Holiday Mission in Nefyn, North Wales) for the many ideas I have picked up there over the years. As an age-group leader, my favourite activity was the 'messy morning' where the children came wearing old clothes and prepared to get themselves very messy! The activities would be set up in advance and small groups of children spent five minutes on each, in a round robin fashion. There was no competitive element. The aim was to get messy and have fun.
Here are some of the things we did. You may wish to use a large plastic sheet or

newspaper, as the floor will soon become very messy! Or better still, play outside. These activities will work best with 8–11 year olds.

you will need...
a large bowl
apples
a sharp knife
towels

80. Apple bobbing

Preparation: cut the apples into quarters; place enough for a small group into the bowl and fill it with water.

The task is for each player to 'bob' for an apple and eat it, using his mouth only. Hands should be held behind the back. This is more difficult than it looks!! Each person can touch only one apple, and don't put apples back for other people to find! Remember to change the water after each small group has played.

> **tip**
> Always have warm soapy water and a towel handy!

you will need...
a baking tray
syrup
cornflakes
a bowl of hot, soapy water
towels

81. Cornflake crazy
Preparation: pour the syrup onto the tray and sprinkle cornflakes on top.
Players should take it in turns to eat the cornflakes out of the syrup. This can also be done with Rolos in honey. Again, change the syrup and cornflakes after each group has played.

you will need...
flour
a bowl
a tray
Smarties
a bowl of hot soapy water
towels

82. The flour game
Preparation: put flour in the bowl, as if you were making a sandcastle, and tip it out onto the tray. Place the Smartie on top.
Each player has to try to take the Smartie from the flour using his mouth only. By now, they may have sticky faces so this could be very messy! Encourage them to eat the Smartie, rather than a mouthful of flour, as this won't be very nice!

you will need...
several colours of paint
plastic trays or plates
paintbrushes
a bowl of warm, soapy water
several towels
a large plastic sheet
large newsprint or wallpaper

83. Foot painting
This is great fun. The children have to step in the paint and walk about on the newsprint, making their mark! They can do the same with handprints too. It is always nice for them to sign their name by their hands or feet when the paint has dried. Remember to wear old clothing and wash afterwards!

> **tip**
> Adults should join in – you have the right to have fun too. If you enjoy and participate in the games, then the children will follow suit.

you will need...
a large number of water bombs

84. Water bombs
Preparation: fill the water bombs with water and put into buckets.
Arrange the group in a circle. Choose one person to be in the middle. The group has to pass the water bomb from the middle to a player, back to the middle and to the next player, back to the middle and so on until it bursts. The team should see how many passes they can make without the bomb bursting, and try to improve their score each time. Make sure that everyone has a go at being in the middle.
You can also play this game with eggs. This is much more expensive but messier and less time-consuming. You could also try putting players into pairs so that they stand opposite each other. Each player can move backwards after each throw to see how far apart they can stand before the water bomb bursts.

you will need...
two buckets
plastic cups with holes in
water

85. There's a hole in my bucket
Set the buckets out, some distance apart. The task is for the whole team to transfer the contents of one bucket into the other using the cups with holes in. They have to lose as little water as possible. The players can either all run at the same time or take it in turns. It is much more crazy and fun

65

when they are all playing at the same time, as water sloshes everywhere! You can also play this game with jelly and spoons. Each team member has to run, with jelly wobbling on their spoon, to put it in a bowl at the other side of the field or yard.

86. Jelly walk

Preparation: put spoonfuls of jelly at intervals all over the plastic sheet.
Split your group up into pairs and number each child 1 or 2. Player number 1 is blindfolded and takes his shoes off. It is the task of player number 2 to guide player 1 across the plastic sheet and to the other side, by shouting directions. Inevitably, player 1 will stand in the jelly at some stage and get very messy!

you will need...
a large plastic sheet
jelly (already made)
blindfolds

87. Balloon shave

Split your group into pairs and number them 1 and 2. Squirt shaving foam all over the balloons. Player 1 holds the balloon in his teeth, and player 2 has to shave the foam off the balloon until it is clean again. When this has been done successfully, let the players swap over.

you will need...
balloons
shaving foam
disposable razors
chairs
newspaper

88. Jammy noses

In New Zealand, people greet friends by rubbing noses with them. Tell the group that they will get to know each other a bit better in this game! Ask your group to stand in a circle, so that they are close together. Put a large blob of jam on the nose of one person in the circle. That

you will need...
jam
paper towels

player then turns to the left and rubs noses with the player standing next to him. The second player then rubs noses with the player to his left, and the nose rubbing continues around the circle until everyone has a jammy nose!

> **tip**
> Remember to play safely and pre-empt any difficult situations: for example, take off children's shoes if necessary, and be careful with furniture or sharp objects.

you will need...
paper plates
paper cups
bowls of water

89. Water tower
The task is for the group to build a tower that is as tall as possible. First, place a cup filled with water onto a paper plate. Then put a plate on top of the cup, and place another water-filled cup on it, then repeat until the tower wobbles and falls over, leaving the players slightly wet!

you will need...
a large pan
porridge
beans
food colouring
other revolting things to put into gunge

90. Gunge tank
This activity is a good one to do at the end of your morning or evening. It is hilarious and the children always love the leader to be gunged. Choose one leader who is game for a laugh, and one child. Each player has to score points by answering questions. The player with the fewest points at the end of the game gets gunged. The funny part is that you always ask the children easy questions, for example, 'what is your name?' and ask the leader difficult questions, for example, 'Name one of Tony Blair's

middle names?' It will always be the leader who is gunged, but you can gunge the child too if they feel left out! Pour the gunge over their heads and listen to the screams!

music games

I could write hundreds of activities involving sound or percussion instruments.
I fully believe that using music is a powerful way of teaching the truth about God and giving children and young people the opportunity to engage with the Bible. We are all innately creative people, as we are made in the image of a creator God. Therefore, when we use creative music, each person is equal and can be equally involved, regardless of any perceived 'talent'; each person is able to create something that is acceptable, as everyone is entitled to their own creative perspective. Therefore confidence grows as children perform to others and receive a response. In performing and composing, they are connecting their innate creativity and spiritualities, so they can learn about God and express themselves to God. I have used music many times as an evangelistic tool, but in such a way that the children and young people have come to learn about God for themselves by being involved in and engaging with a Bible passage or story. I recommend you to 'have a go' even if you have no or few instruments, or even if you feel shy of music! It's great fun and the children will enjoy it. Percussion instruments that you might like to have in your stock

are: rain sticks; finger cymbals; claves and woodblocks; cymbals; chime bars; a tambourine; a tambour; a drum; a triangle and, if possible, a glockenspiel or xylophone. It can be an expensive task to build up a set of instruments, but if they are looked after well, they will last for a long time and provide an amazing wealth of opportunity for co-operative activity. But you can also make sounds using your body, or found sounds (sounds found in the environment). You will be surprised what effects you can make by rustling empty crisp packets, tearing newspaper and hitting or shaking a Pringles tube (empty or full!). Before attempting to make creative music with the children, I like to play games with them so that they can familiarise themselves with the instruments, learn how to control them and how to work together. Here are a handful of group activities which explore sound, and encourage co-operation.

> **tip**
> The term 'texture' in music refers to the number of players performing at one time – everyone together, or just one or two musicians.

91. Absence of sound
Ask the children to put their fingers in their ears and listen to the absence of sound. What does it feel like? What would the world be like without sound?

92. Hand band
Each person can produce a sound by using parts of their body. It could be a finger click, leg slap, pop in cheek, click of the tongue, etc. Choose a conductor to direct the performance. Each player should perform the sound when the conductor points at him. He may point to individuals or groups of people. Explore the variety of sounds that can be made. The same activity can be done using *vocal sounds*, such as whee, hum, aahh, etc.

93. Sound collage
Ask the children to investigate the sounds they can make with their instruments, bodies, or found sounds. Experiment with combinations of sounds, and explore different textures. In the group, or in small groups, put together a sound collage. This could be based on a stimulus (for example, a poem or a picture), or it could simply be a collection of sounds.

94. Chance music

Each person uses an instrument, body or found sound to compose a short pattern. The leader begins the piece by performing his pattern. Then each player performs their own pattern at random, up to three times each. Sometimes two or more may clash, but as the sound of the music is complete chance, this can bring about a variety of textures, dynamics and even silence. It produces an interesting effect. It is good for players to listen, and to try to play at appropriate times. This also facilitates concentration.

you will need...
cards showing pictures of the instruments

95. Flash cards

Group the players according to the sound quality of their instrument, for example all the scratching sounds together, all the banging sounds, all the tinkling sounds. The leader has a selection of flash cards which she holds up to direct play. Therefore, when a picture of a triangle is held up, all the instruments in the triangle's group will play. One or more flash cards can be held up simultaneously, to give a variety of sounds.

96. Billy Beater

All players have an instrument. When Billy Beater (i.e. a beater or pencil) is on the floor, there is silence. As Billy is lifted up from the floor, the players begin to play, quietly at first and progressively more loudly as the beater gets higher, and they grow quieter as the beater gets lower. This encourages them to work together to achieve a common effect, but also means that they have to watch very carefully to respond accordingly. Watch that they don't get faster as they get louder!

97. Musical Mexican wave
The players sit in a circle, and a leader stands in the middle. The leader points to each player in the circle with the beater, one at a time. As they do so, the player plays a sound. The leader can go around the circle quickly or slowly, so the players have to be alert and ready to play! You get a Mexican wave effect, and it is fun!

98. Hide the beater
Let the children take it in turns to hide a beater anywhere in the room. Meanwhile another child, or pair, leave the room, so they don't know where the beater is. When they return, they have to find the beater by following musical instructions given by the other players. When the group plays quietly, the players are a long way from the beater, but as they move nearer to it, the group will play more and more loudly until the beater is found.

99. Group rondo
A *rondo* is a piece of music which has the structure: A B A C A.
The children split up into groups A, B and C according to the quality of sound that they can make, for example all tapping

instruments go in group A, all vocal sounds in group B and all jangling sounds in group C. Hold cards up saying A, B, C in the rondo order and the children play when their card is held. You can ask them to play loudly or quietly, quickly or slowly in order to bring more variety to the piece. As A plays more times than B and C, children will all want to be in group A. To make it fair, rename the groups each time you play, so that each group has had an opportunity to be A.

A good extension activity is to listen to *Rondo al Turka* by Mozart, or many Beatles songs, and try to identify parts A, B and C by holding up the cards when they are played.

100. Contrasts
Ask the children to investigate ways of playing the instruments that will provide contrasts. They can do these in small groups or pairs. The contrasts can be simple at first, for example, fast/slow; loud/quiet. Then they can progress to rough/smooth, mellow/excited, war/peace, summer/winter, working in groups as they get to know the instruments better. Allow time for discussion in the activity time as they will need to talk and evaluate their work.

101. Obwisanna
This is an African rock-passing game which can be played equally by passing claves (sticks). Teach the children the

song and sing it several times until they are comfortable with it. Then sing the song and clap along to the pulse (i.e. clap on every other beat: on Ob-, Sa, Ob-, Sa, Ob-, Sa, Ob-, Sa). The next step is to do a kind of Mexican wave. Rather than clapping, the children lift their arms on the first beat and then lower them on the second beat. This will reinforce their sense of pulse.

The game can really start when you introduce the claves, but don't progress to this until you are confident that the children have grasped the concept of pulse.

When you introduce the claves, set them in front of you. The task is to send the claves around the circle in time to the song, each child having a go. On **Ob-,** grab hold of the claves, one in each hand. On **Sa**, lift them into the air. On the next **Ob-**, place the claves in front of the person to your right, so that on **Sa,** they will lift them into the air, and on the next **Ob-,** they will in turn place the claves in front of the person on their right. See how far around the circle you can get. If it goes wrong at any time, carry on until you reach the end of the song, stop and try again. It is difficult, but a great group challenge, which is fun whether attained or not. You can extend the activity by introducing more claves starting at different places in the circle and perhaps even moving in the opposite direction!

Obwisanna

Ob - wi - san - na sa na na Ob - wi - san - na sa

Ob - wi - san - na sa na na Ob - wi - san - na sa.

© 1999 Scripture Union

102. Sound dominoes

Give the children an instrument each and ask them to experiment with the sound it makes and to choose a way of playing it. Alternatively, if you don't have instruments, ask them to choose a body sound eg clapping/clicking. The leader may give examples. They will work individually for this game.

Sit the children in a circle and one at a time ask them to perform their sound. You could even go around the circle a couple of times. The task is for the children to place themselves in such an order that their sounds correspond. To play, choose a child to perform his or her sound. That child can stand in the middle of the room to begin the dominoes game. He then chooses another group member to stand next to him. The second person must have a sound that is similar to the first person's sound. The second person then also chooses someone to stand next to him. Each person can choose to change the direction of the line at any time, just as in real dominoes. When there are no more sounds that would fit, start again, the first person in the next group choosing a new place to stand and starting a new line.

When all the children have been given places, listen to the collective sound of each group. Ask the children to describe the sounds and what they remind them of. This is a great introductory activity for letting children explore how they can make sounds, and can be a good way of leading into musical composition.

103. All change
Sit the group in a circle. Each child chooses a sound by experimenting with an instrument or body sound as above. The leader also has a selection of instruments which corresponds to that of the group. Choose a child to sit in the centre of the circle without an instrument. When the leader plays a sound on an instrument or body part, all the children who have a similar-sounding sound source run into the centre of the circle and find a new place. The child in the centre also runs to a new place. There should be one child left in the middle, who then gives their instrument to the person who was previously in the middle. This game is

good fun, as there is no winner or loser, but excitement is created as players scramble for places. It also allows children to play different instruments, as the group becomes mixed up when the person in the middle changes.

104. Rainstorm
Players split into groups and each group chooses a body or vocal sound pattern to represent a part of a rainstorm: patter of raindrops; beginning to rain; wind blowing up; full storm. Perform each section, building up layers of sound until the full storm is performed, and then die away to silence.

105. Weather forecast
An extension of this activity, if you have instruments, is to create a musical weather forecast. Make weather symbols like those on the weather forecast to use as visual stimuli and ask the children to create sound effects to represent each type of weather; for example, the sun could be played by a choice of tinkling instruments such as finger cymbals and triangles; the wind could be represented by a cymbal roll, a rain stick being rattled, or a quieter drum roll. You could even get a map of the country, stick the weather symbols on it, and as you give your weather forecast the children could play their sounds.

> **tip**
> Remember that rules are important when playing with instruments. When you are speaking, the children should always have their instruments on the floor, away from their fidgety fingers!

106. Play a picture

Many works by modern artists are perfect as stimuli for creative music. Wassily Kandinsky painted works with many colours and unusual shapes, and Paul Klee used bold strong lines and shapes. Modern Art calendars are popular, and can be found in the shops in the months leading up to Christmas. I buy one every Christmas, focusing on a different artist each year. I then have a stock ready to be performed!

Look closely at the shapes in the picture. How does the artist use colour, line and texture? How can these be represented in sound? Play in response to the picture. You may want to contrast the bold and bright effects of Kandinsky with the softer, more mellow works of Van Gogh or Monet. Impressionist artists would blur their outlines and paint using variations on one or two colours to achieve their effects. The musical interpretations could reflect this. You could even listen to music by Debussy, Ravel or Satie, to show how the composers did a similar thing. Try using Asian or Oriental art for the same activity, but a different effect. You could try a variety of stimuli and discuss with the children how each produced a different effect.

107. Sad and happy faces

In a circle, ask the children to brainstorm all the emotions that they experience day by day. Then ask them to explain which experiences may have led them to feel these emotions (for example, happy, sad, proud, angry, etc). You can draw these faces onto card circles to use as visual stimuli.

Then listen to pieces of music that represent emotions, for example, 'Death of Åse' from *Peer Gynt* by Grieg (sad); 'Anitra's dance' from *Peer Gynt* by Grieg (happy); the theme from the 'Pathetique' sonata or the 'Appassionata' sonata by Beethoven (excited/worried); 'The Great Gate of Kiev' from the work *Pictures at an Exhibition* by Mussorgsky (proud); the overture from the *Marriage of Figaro* by Mozart (excited).

In small groups, ask the children to investigate how they can play their instruments so as to represent these emotions. Slow and quiet playing sounds sad, and fast, energetic playing sounds excited. This activity is a great discussion starter which may lead to further discussion and also perhaps prayer as children open up about their feelings in a safe and creative context.

108. Sound effects

Many Bible stories can be told using sound effects which highlight certain parts of the story, or provide an accompaniment to the reading. I am an advocate of children learning through experience. In creating music, children are entering the world of the story. They engage with the events and characters, which may lead to discussion. The power and nature of God is also revealed through many stories. Creating sounds to represent the nature of God can be a very simple yet profound way of discovering more about Him.

> **tip**
> Read a Bible story several times before attempting a composition. Use a couple of different versions, if possible.

Good Bible passages for creative music are:
Genesis 1 – the story of Creation
Exodus 3 and 4 – Moses at the burning bush
1 Kings 18 and 19 – Elijah: the battle with

the prophets of Baal and then the 'still small voice'
Daniel 3 – the fiery furnace
Lamentations 4 – this is full of contrasts
Ecclesiastes 3
Psalms 8 and 148
Acts 1:6–10 – the ascension of Jesus
Acts 2 – the coming of the Holy Spirit
Mark 4 – the parable of the sower
Mark 4:35–41 – Jesus calms the storm
Revelation 21 – the glory of heaven.
Here is my paraphrased version of the story of Moses at the burning bush, with ideas for how to use instruments in telling the story.

Moses
One day, Moses was taking care of his father-in-law's sheep and goats. He led the flock across the desert and came to Mount Sinai, the holy mountain. There, an **angel** *(use tinkling instruments such as a triangle, finger cymbals and chime bars, played slowly and quietly)* of the Lord appeared to him as a **flame** *(use scratching instruments such as egg shakers, scrapers, sand block or rain maker)* coming to him from the middle of a bush. Moses saw that the bush was on fire but **was not burning up** *(use instruments as for the flame, but get louder, and increase the number of instruments playing, to make a full sound)*. He went closer to look, and God called to him from the bush: '**Moses! Moses! You are on holy ground. I have**

seen how my people are being treated cruelly in Egypt and I am sending you to the king of Egypt so that you can lead my people out of this country' *(use a drum, cymbal, or any other instrument that will create a powerful and strong sound in the background)*. Moses was afraid, and doubted that the Israelites would believe him. God said, **'throw the stick you are holding to the ground'** *(use instruments that make a clicking sound, for example, claves or a woodblock)*. Moses did so and it **turned into a snake** *(use small scratching instruments such as egg shakers or maracas)*. Then God said, 'pick it up now, by the tail.' Moses did so, and it **turned back into a stick** *(use clicking instruments, as above)*. God then told Moses to do this to prove to the Israelites that the Lord, the God of Abraham, Isaac and Jacob had appeared to him.

parachute games

The parachute is a brilliant way of facilitating co-operation amongst your group, since most games involve players working together as a team. I always begin a parachute session with an opportunity to shake the parachute as hard as they can, to let off some energy. They will be desperate to shake it, so this will get it out of their system before beginning to play games.

> **tip**
> Before playing with the parachute, go over the rules. I tell children that they must not wear shoes for safety reasons; they must not put their hand through the hole in the middle, and they must not shake the parachute while anyone is talking. With these rules in mind, you will have a great time.

109. Mushroom
A lot of games use this action, so it's good to practise first. All players work together by bending down with the parachute, then lifting up. They keep hold of the parachute so that it forms a dome-like shape. Do this several times. To play the game, go

down and up three times. Then, after going down and up for the third time, keep hold of the parachute in the air and everyone runs into the middle so that it becomes like a big mushroom. You can also let it fall on the children by telling them to let go, as they will enjoy scrambling out of it.

110. Under the sea
All players lift the parachute together by bending their legs, going down first and then stretching up. Then send half the children to lie down on their backs underneath the parachute with their arms and legs on the floor. The remaining players are to lift the parachute up and down five times altogether so that they make a wind for the resting players. This is really good fun. Make sure that everyone has a go, especially the leaders!

111. Up and under
Everyone helps to work the parachute by bending down then up, simultaneously, three times. After the third time, the leader calls for players to change places, for example:
If you play a musical instrument, change!
If you are wearing blue, change!
The children then run under the parachute and find a new place. Play until everyone has had a go.

you will need...
a ball

112. Mexican wave
Place a ball on the parachute. The group must make the ball roll around the edge of the parachute by making a Mexican wave and all working together. It's OK if the ball rolls off the parachute. Just put it back on, and see if the group can keep it going for longer next time!

you will need...
a ball

113. In the hole
In a similar fashion to the previous game, lift and tilt the parachute so that a ball is directed towards the hole in the middle. The players must work together as a team to get the ball to rest on the centre hole for three seconds.

you will need...
a ball

114. Making waves
By making waves with the parachute, see how long the ball can be kept up in the air without falling off or going over the edge. Give yourselves a target, for example, one minute and then see if you can beat your group record.

115. Birthday present
Wrap players up in the parachute, pretending that they are a birthday present. Sing 'Happy birthday!' You can also use a Christmas carol at Christmas. The task is for the players to scramble out of the parachute before the end of the song.

116. Climb the mountain
Choose two children to climb the mountain. Players make a mushroom, but all players must be kneeling down. Pull the edges of the mushroom towards the ground so the parachute makes a bubble and the two chosen players scramble across the parachute mountain as fast as they can.

117. Sea storm
Select two players to lie down in the middle of the parachute. Everyone else shakes the parachute so that it makes waves around them. This is a lovely activity for younger children who respond to touch and the senses.

118. Turtle
Imagine that the parachute is the shell of a turtle. All the players hold the parachute above them, facing outwards, and then get underneath. The task is then for the whole group to move in one direction, making sure that the shell never loses its shape. An extension activity is to put obstacles in the way of the 'turtle', for the group to manoeuvre round or climb over, still making sure that the shell doesn't lose its shape.

119. Sharks
Select a child to be the shark and send them under the parachute. Everyone except the shark sits around the parachute holding it to their waist with their legs underneath. The shark under

the parachute crawls around and pulls screaming people by their legs under the parachute. Once they are under the parachute, they too become sharks until the whole group is underneath the parachute. You can play this game until everyone has had a chance to be the first shark.

you will need...
a box with household items

120. Hidden treasure

Select a player to be the diver. Put various articles and oddments into a treasure box under the parachute. The group makes waves using the parachute and the diver has to retrieve as many items as he can from under the chute, one by one. Again each child should have the chance to be the diver.

121. Hidden shoes

This is a variation on the game above. All the children take off their shoes and throw them underneath the parachute. A leader then goes underneath and mixes up all the shoes. The children then stand up around the parachute and walk around clockwise until the leader tells them to stop. They are now in a different position from before. On the count of three, the children scramble underneath the parachute to retrieve their shoes. Mayhem normally ensues, but there is no winner. The game is over when the last person has his shoes back on his feet where they belong.

> **tip**
> Think: have I explained the game clearly? Does everybody understand what they have to do?

122. Cat and mouse
I think this must be one of the most popular parachute games, but it is most effective when your parachute is not transparent. Also, please don't play this outside on a hard surface (as I learnt to my cost). The result was a very 'holey' parachute and some scratched knees. Select one player to be the cat and another to be the mouse. The mouse goes under the parachute and the others hide him by shaking the parachute very hard. Meanwhile, let the cat sit on top of the parachute (without shoes on!). The cat must chase the mouse and catch him as quickly as possible.

you will need...
a ball

123. Parachute volleyball
If you have two parachutes, this game is wonderful for older children and enables them to work together. Split your group into two. Each half takes hold of a parachute. The task is to send a ball from one parachute to the other, as in volleyball. This is not as easy as it sounds, but most teams do eventually come up with a strategy that works.

124. Tent
The group makes a mushroom and then each player puts the parachute over their head, under their bottom, and sits on it! Under the parachute you can tell stories, sing songs and tell jokes.

125. Parachute prayers
Make a mushroom and, while underneath, children can say a prayer. When they have done that, repeat the game, so that you allow children some time to think about how they want to pray.

> **tip**
>
> It is fun to go underneath the parachute, but make each 'visit' short, as it gets hot very quickly, and the children need fresh air.

126. Parachute Bible stories
It is great fun to use the parachute to tell Bible stories. It is also a wonderful way to enable the children to participate in the story in a memorable way.

Here are some of my ideas for using the parachute in storytelling.

Jesus calms the storm (Mark 4:35–41)
(Children hold the parachute still.) On the evening of that same day Jesus said to his disciples, 'Let us go across to the other side of the lake.' So they left the crowd; the disciples got into the boat in which Jesus was already sitting, and they

took him with them. **(Shake the parachute very gently, to represent the lake.)** Other boats were there too. Suddenly a strong wind blew up and the waves began to spill over the boat, so that it was about to fill with water. **(Shake the parachute harder now so that it balloons and forms a wind.)** Jesus was in the back of the boat, sleeping with his head on a pillow. The disciples woke him up and said 'teacher, don't you care that we are about to die?'

Jesus stood up and commanded the wind, 'Be quiet!' and he said to the waves, 'Be still!' The wind died down, and there was great calm. **(Stop shaking the parachute and hold it still.)** Then Jesus said to his disciples, 'Why are you frightened? Have still no faith?'

But they were terribly afraid and said to one another, 'Who is this man? Even the wind and waves obey him!'

Jonah

There was once a man called Jonah. One day God spoke to him and told him to go to a place called Nineveh. The people there were wicked, so Jonah set off in the opposite direction to get away from God. He went to Joppa, where he found a ship that was about to go to Spain. He went on board and the ship set off. **(All shake the parachute gently to represent the ship on the sea.)** But God sent a strong wind on the sea **(shake the parachute slightly harder)** and then a storm broke

(shake the parachute even harder) so that the ship was in danger of breaking up **(run with the parachute from side to side, shaking it hard at the same time)**. The sailors were terrified and cried out for help **(all shout 'help!')**. Jonah knew that they were in danger because he had disobeyed God. He told them what he had done, and so the sailors picked up Jonah and threw him into the sea. As soon as they had done that, the sea calmed down **(stop shaking and hold the parachute still)**. But at God's command a big fish came along and swallowed Jonah **(all pull the parachute over heads and sit on it)**. Inside the belly of the fish, Jonah said sorry to God that he had disobeyed him and promised that he would obey him in future. After three days and three nights, God made the fish spit Jonah onto the shore **(all come out of the parachute)**. God then told Jonah to go to Nineveh. This time Jonah obeyed God and went to tell the people the message about God **(all shake the parachute gently one last time)**.

> **tip**
>
> There are different sizes of parachute available. Choose one which is appropriate to the age of the children in your group and the size of the group. Large parachutes are great but can be difficult to manage with a smaller group.

The Creation

This is a dance to the reading of the story of Creation and involves a parachute. I have used music by Stravinsky – *The Rite of Spring* – as an accompaniment, but it can also be done unaccompanied.

Place the parachute on the floor in the middle of the room and when you come to the following phrases use the action provided

'All was dark, quiet and still' – all children lie very still on the floor.

'Power of God moving over the water' – one child travels in and out of the others, on tiptoes, slowly and quickly, high and low.

'Let there be light!' – children 'wake up' and begin to move, jumping up and down and moving quickly.

'Let there be a dome to divide the water' – all pick up the parachute and make a 'mushroom'.

'The water He named sea' – make a sea effect by shaking the parachute.

'Plants which grow' – lay the parachute down and all take different levels and grow upwards or outwards using the fingertips first and stretching out.

'Sun, moon and stars' – all hold the

parachute for the sun by holding it tight and walking it around in a circle. Then lay it flat and all stretch out with feet on the edge of the parachute, to represent the stars.

'The air be filled with birds' – children to be birds and animals and swoop around the space.

'God created human beings' – all hold hands and circle the parachute. Stay linked in circle to end.

running games

127. Your number's up!
Players run around the room until a number is called by the leader. They then team up with other players so that they form a group the size of that number. Play the game quickly so that no one stays 'out', and those left over from one round are soon in another group. One variation is to call out the names of shapes, for example, 'square of eight' or 'circle of six'.

128. Chain tig
Select one player. He runs around and chases the others. When he has 'tigged' someone, the 'tigged' person then 'tigs' another and they join hands to form a chain. They continue to chase and add other players to the chain until all players are in the chain.

129. Popcorn
A similar idea to the above. The players move around the room and when they choose, become popcorn and pop (i.e. jump into the air). If they touch another player they then stick together and try to stick to others. But they must be careful not to bang into other players and get hurt.

> **tip**
> Frequently change the person who is 'it', as this player will get tired easily. Also you want to give as many children as possible the chance to have a go.

130. Nintendo touch
Each player has five lives. Select one player to run around and chase the others. When 'tigged', players lose a life and keep losing lives until they have no lives left. When no lives are left, that player then becomes a 'tigger'.

131. Stuck in the mud/Snowmen

Select one player to run around and chase the others. When caught, players stand with their arms and legs stretched out, and they are released when another player runs under their arm or crawls through their legs. One variation is that, when caught, players freeze like a statue until they are touched by another player, which unfreezes them, so they can join in again.

132. Duck and goose

Players sit in a circle. One player is selected to walk around the outside of the circle and tap each player on the head, saying, 'duck, duck, duck'. However, when he says 'goose!' to one player, that player has to chase the first player round the circle and back to the empty space. If he is not caught, the first caller has another go. If he is, there is a new caller. Play until everyone has had a go.

133. Budge

Put newspaper or mats around the room to act as 'dens'. Alternatively, you can use pillars or sections of wall to be dens. In this game, one person is 'it' and they must 'tig' another player. When 'tigged', that player is then 'it.' However, players can only be 'tigged' when running between dens. At any time a player can go to a den where they will be safe. But only one person is allowed at a den at one time, so a player already in a den can be removed from it by another player shouting 'budge!' That player then has to join in the running to avoid being 'tigged'. As this is hard work for the person who is 'it', you may want to stop the game every so often to give players a breather!

134. Baked beans
Someone shouts out the names of all the different beans (see below). Children have to make a noise or do an action appropriate for each different type of bean:
Runner bean – run on the spot
Jumping bean – jump
String bean – make yourself as tall as you can
Chilli bean – shiver as if you are cold
Mexican bean – act as if you are too hot
Broad bean – make yourself as wide as you can
When the caller shouts out, 'Baked beans!', everyone runs to touch the nearest wall.

135. Traffic lights

This game is very similar to Baked beans. Children run around the room, but follow your instructions. When you call out 'Red!', they stop; 'Amber!', they walk about; and 'Green!', they run about. You can change the meanings of the colours to make the game more interesting.

136. Rats and rabbits

Split the players into two groups. The groups stand in rows facing each other. One row is called *rats*, the other *rabbits*. When the caller shouts *rats*, the rats chase the rabbits to a line or a wall, or when *rabbits* is called, the rabbits chase the rats to the line. If a player is caught before reaching the line, they join the opposite team.

> **tip**
>
> Never make a big issue about keeping score, or saying who has won and who has lost. If a game does involve scoring, throw numbers at random, for example '567 to you and 598 to you'. The children will scream and shout at you, but it is funny. They won't be able to keep up with your hilarious scoring method, and you keep control!

137. Cat and mouse

Children line up in several rows with their arms outstretched. One person is the cat and another is the mouse. The mouse runs up and down the rows. The cat is then sent to chase it. They must not break through outstretched arms. Each time the leader shouts 'change', the children must turn to face sideways, thus barring the way and making the cat and mouse change direction. Once the cat has caught the mouse, a new cat and mouse are chosen.

138. Story time

The players sit in a circle or a line and are given the names of characters in a story. The caller tells the story and, when a character's name is called, the players with that name run around the circle or to a given line. The story could be, for example, about a trip to the zoo, where the characters are the names of the family or the animals. When *the family* is called or *the animals*, then all players run.

This is my version of this game using the Christmas story (adapted from the *Good News Bible*). The names in bold are the characters; people chosen to be those characters have to run when their name is called.

Luke 2:8–20

There were some **shepherds** in that part of the country who were spending the night in the fields, taking care of their flocks. An **angel** of the Lord appeared to them and the glory of the Lord appeared over them. They were terribly afraid, but the **angel** said to them, 'Don't be afraid! I am here with good news for you, which will bring great joy to all the people. This very day in David's town your Saviour was born – Christ the Lord! And this is what will prove it to you: you will find a baby wrapped in strips of cloth and lying in a **manger**.'

Suddenly a great army of heaven's **angels** appeared with the **angel**, singing praises to **God**:

'Glory to **God** in the highest heaven, and peace on earth to those with whom he is pleased!'

When the **angels** went away from them back into heaven, the **shepherds** said to one another, 'Let's go to **Bethlehem** and see this thing that has happened, which the Lord has told us.'

So they hurried off and found **Mary** and **Joseph** and saw the baby lying in the **manger**. When the **shepherds** saw him, they told them what the **angel** had said about the child. All who heard it were amazed at what the **shepherds** said.

Mary remembered all these things and thought deeply about them. The **shepherds** went back, singing praises to **God** for all they had heard and seen; it had been just as the **angel** had told them.

> **tip**
>
> Remember to frequently ask the children: 'Who hasn't had a chance to be "it" yet?' You want to be fair. Some children will be quiet and may end up not taking part, if you don't ask!

139. All the fish in the sea

All players stand in a circle. A variation on Story time is to give each child the name of a fish, from a choice of four: for example cod, plaice, haddock, shrimp. When their fish name is called, players run around the circle. When the caller shouts *'tide turns'* they go in the opposite direction. When *'there's a storm!'* is called, they run faster, and when *'shark attack!'* is called, they all pretend to be sharks. When *'tide's coming in'* is called, players go back to their place. A shout of *'all the fish in the sea!'* means that all the players must run.

you will need...
several pots of play bubbles; food colouring

140. Bubbles
The players line up in two lines as two teams. They choose a 'blower' to blow for that team (each bubble pot contains different-coloured food colouring). They blow the bubbles and each team has to collectively waft the bubbles using newspaper towards the other side of the room in a given time.

141. Captain's on board
I have been playing this game for years, but it is a good one. If you speed up the instruction calling, the play will become fast and furious and much more fun as the players try to keep up.

Name the four walls in your venue: *North, East, South* and *West*. When you call out each name, the players run to the appropriate wall. There are additional instructions to call, for example, *'climb the rigging'* (the players mime a climbing action, or climb wallbars if you have them); *'scrub the decks'* (players go on their hands and knees and pretend to scrub the floor); *'sharks coming'* (players put a hand on their head to pretend to be a shark, and sing the *Jaws* theme tune); *'man overboard'* (players lie on their backs with one leg in the air); and *'Captain's on board'* (players stand to attention and salute). There are no winners and losers in this game. Just keep the children active and involved, and you will wear them out!

142. Mouse tails

you will need...
pieces of string, enough for each player to have one

Give each player a piece of string and ask them to stick it in the back of their shoe, so that some of the string is sticking out. The players must chase each other around the room, and stand on each other's 'tails.' The string should come out of the shoe when stood on. The game is over when everyone has lost their tails. As a variation, you may want to tie a balloon to players' legs. The players then burst each other's balloons.

tip
Safety is very important. Make sure that you set out any rules with the children before you play fast games, particularly rules about touching.

team-building games

Team-building games are excellent for developing communication skills with people in your group. Many of the following activities require strategy planning, thought, discussion and, ultimately, teamwork. The tasks cannot be completed without the involvement of the whole group. Such tasks are also an excellent opportunity for group members to display hidden talents, and learn more about each other. A group discussion can take place afterwards as the members reflect on what they have learnt from the games.

143. One man and his dog

Set up a simple obstacle course. One team member is nominated to be the caller. The others are to be blindfolded and hold hands. They are the 'sheep'. The caller must direct the 'sheep' around the course by hand claps or vocal sounds. However, in preparation, the team need to spend 10 minutes together to work on a strategy for planning. For example, one clap means go straight ahead; two claps mean go right and three claps mean go left. A whistle could mean to turn round.

Teams should work out their own ideas! To play the game, the sheep must stick closely together and listen to the caller's instructions. To make it more difficult, the 'sheep' could all be scattered around the room and before completing the course, first have to find each other. That will take some serious strategy planning!

144. Co-op letters
It's fun to make letters and words using your body. In a group, make the longest word you can – this has to be able to be read by the leader.

you will need...
a bunch of keys

145. Keys of the kingdom
The aim of the game is for a pair of players (who are blindfolded and perhaps even three-legged) to be directed through a maze of stationary people to a set of keys which they need to pick up. You will need the pair, a player to give directions and the remaining group members can form the human maze. When the first pair have completed the task, swap jobs around so that each group member has had an opportunity to take each part.

146. Log roll
Tell the group to lie on the floor alongside each other on mats and all to roll together along the mats, in synchronisation, working as a team. Practise this a few times before attempting the task – which is to load one or two players on top of the group so that

when the group roll, the 'logs' are rolled along their backs!

147. Amoebas

Group members face outwards and all link arms. The task is for the whole team to complete an obstacle course without breaking the chain.

> **tip**
>
> To add excitement, create a game where the children work together against an imaginary outside force, against the clock, or even the leader. The focus will then shift away from competition between themselves.

148. Skin the snake

The players line up, so that they are all standing behind another player. Each player puts his right hand through his legs to link with the left hand of the player behind, who has stretched her left hand out in front of her. The player at the back of the line, who should really be the smallest player (but the group can work this out for themselves!) then kneels down and crawls through the legs of the penultimate player, still holding hands. This player then crawls through the legs of the rest of the line, taking the others through with them. The task is for the whole team to go through all the legs in one continuous line without letting go of each other's hands.

149. Knotty problem
Ask the team to form a circle and to stretch out their arms in front of them. Each player then grabs two other hands at random, so that a knot forms. The task is to unravel the knot without letting go. If the task is completed quickly, do it again, It might not be so easy next time!

you will need...
newspaper
scissors
string
Creme egg or similar item

150. Bridge building
Give each group some newspaper, string and Sellotape. They are to design and make a structure that will hold the weight of a Creme egg or similar item. Again, give them time to talk through their strategy and then give them 10 minutes in which to build their structure.

151. Tallest tower
As a variation on the above game, see which group can build the tallest tower. The group will have to decide on a strategy for building upwards when the tower is taller than the tallest person in the group.

you will need...
an old drainpipe
a drill
a plank of wood
a ping-pong ball
a bucket
water

152. Ping-pong crazy

Preparation: take an old drainpipe or part of a drainpipe and drill holes into it. Fix the drainpipe onto a piece of wood or some other sort of base and put a ping-pong ball in the pipe.

The task is for the team to get the ball out of the pipe without touching it. They can use water, but should remember that it will come out of the holes quite quickly!

It's best to play this outside – you will get wet!

you will need...
a hoop
a milk bottle
three skipping ropes
elastic

153. Bottle pick up
This game is on a similar theme to Ping pong crazy. Put the bottle inside the hoop. The task is to use the elastic and rope in order to get the bottle out of the hoop, without touching the bottle with your hands! Inside the hoop is a no-go area: no one is allowed to go in or they may be sucked up!

you will need...
rope or bungee cord

154. Spider's web
Preparation: using a large wooden frame or two strong trees, make a large spider's web. You can do this by tying bungee cord or thick rope to the frame or tree and then weaving a pattern as shown in the illustration on the next page.
The task is to 'post' your team through the web, using any of the holes. You can say that the web is made of electrified barbed wire and so must not be touched under any circumstances! Each team member is allowed to come back through the web, but must also go back in the same way and so this may slow down the task. The task is complete when the whole team has been 'posted' through.

155. Crossing the poisoned river

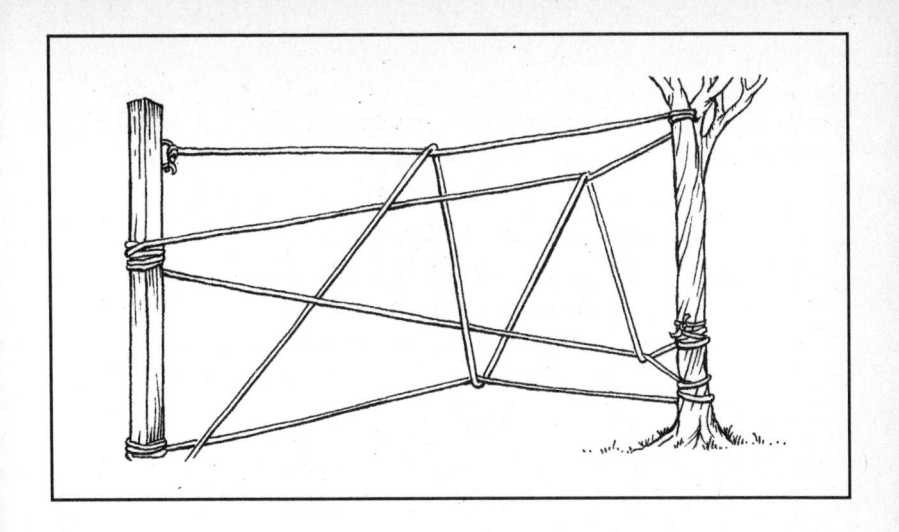

you will need...
crash mats
rugs or
newspaper

Give each team two big mats or two chairs. The task is for the whole team to cross over the floor (the poisoned river) from A to B without anyone's feet touching the floor. Several teams can do this at the same time, but it is not a race. The teams can spread out in the room or even use different rooms as they devise their strategy, and then after 10 or so minutes ask each team in turn to show the others how they completed the task.

156. Electric fence

you will need...
two poles and a
piece of rope or
string

Preparation: tie the rope between the two poles, about four feet off the floor.
The object of the game is for the entire team to get over the 'electric fence' (the rope) without getting 'electrocuted' (touching the rope). Each team member goes one at a time, with or without help from his team-mates. What makes this

game interesting is that even though one player goes over the rope at a time, the other team members can help in any way they want. Once a person is over the fence, however, he must stay over the fence and not come back around to help anyone else. So the last person in each team must somehow get over the fence without help from the other side. This game requires lots of teamwork and co-operation!

group activities

The following activities can be played by your whole group, or in smaller groups within the whole. The task is for the group itself, so be careful not to encourage competition between groups. Many of these activities can also be done with all age groups, fostering a family feel in your event.

you will need...
a blanket

157. Who is it?
Split the group into two smaller groups. Each small group stands facing each other with a blanket to separate them. Each group nominates a player to stand directly in front of the blanket. When the blanket is dropped, each player says the name of the person facing them. The first person to say the name then takes the other to his side.
Play until everyone has had a go, or one side has won all the players.

you will need...
balloons
water pistols

158. Balloon bash
A balloon is thrown into the room. The group must, collectively, keep the balloon in the air using hands, blowing or water pistols. Time how long the balloon is kept in the air and try to beat the group record.

you will need...
flour
a bowl
Smarties
a bowl of warm water
a towel
paper towels
a knife

159. Birthday cake
Make a cake by putting flour in a bowl and tipping it upside down. Place a Smartie on top of the cake. In turn, the players take a slice out of the cake, trying to stop the Smartie from falling off. When the Smartie eventually falls off, the player who made it fall has to pick it out of the flour with his teeth!

you will need...
a ball of string

160. Spider's web talk time
All players sit in a circle. The leader holds the end of a ball of string. He then throws the ball to another player and says something positive to that person, for example, 'you are kind.' That player then holds the string, and throws the ball to another player, also saying something positive to that person. Play until everyone has had a couple of goes. Then, pull the string tightly and you will see that a spider's web has been formed while all players have been affirming each other! They can also talk about pertinent issues. The children at 'Powerpack' have voted this game as the 'best game of all time!' I think it is because it creates an opportunity to talk in a safe environment, and a sense of wonder at the web which is spun before their eyes as they play.

you will need...
hula-hoops
a CD player
CDs

161. Musical hoops
Spread hula-hoops on the floor and play lively, fun music. When the music stops, each player has to run to stand inside a hoop. At no time must any player stand outside a hoop when the music has stopped. Repeat, but each time the music plays, remove a hoop so that when there are no longer enough hoops for each person to have one each, players will have to share. Eventually three, four or five players may be sharing a hoop, but remember: no one is allowed to touch the floor! The game ends when there is no way for the players to safely stay in the remaining hoops.

> **tip**
> Physical games are good for legitimising and encouraging 'safe' touch.

you will need...
a long piece of string or rope
blindfolds

162. Blind square
Ask the players to stand in a circle and give them a circle of rope. Each player must hold the rope with at least one hand. Then blindfold all the players. The task is for the group to form a square out of the rope, but without being able to see what they are doing. When the group think they have completed the task, remove the blindfolds where they are so they can see what they have done. You can repeat this game asking them to form other shapes such as triangles, hexagons and pentagons! It is also good to have a

discussion time afterwards about what it was like not being able to see. This can then lead into the story of the healing of Bartimaeus.

163. Musical jigsaws

you will need...
a magazine

Preparation: cut up pictures from the magazine into three or four pieces so that there are enough pieces for each player to have one piece.

Play loud and lively music and the children can dance. When the music stops, each player grabs the player closest to him to see if their jigsaw pieces match up. If they do, the pair stay together and try to find the players with the rest of their jigsaw. If not, continue playing the game. The game ends when the whole group has matched up their jigsaws.

164. An arty problem

you will need...
a picture
photocopies of the picture
felt-tip pens or paints
newspaper
water
paintbrushes

Preparation: take a copy of a famous painting, or an image that relates to your theme and, using the photocopier, enlarge it so that you have about four sections which, stuck together, would recreate the image.

Hand out the photocopies to the children, either one each or one to each group, depending on the number of children you have. The task is to copy that part of the picture and to paint it so that the representation is as close to the original as possible. When each section is finished, stick them all together to make your own group version of the picture, but four times as big!

you will need...
paper bricks
pens

165. Writing wall
Cut out 'bricks' from paper. Have two 'walls', one saying *I can*, the other *You can*. Write or draw about yourself and the things you can do. Also write or draw about another person and the things they can do well. Encourage each other in the things you write.

you will need...
paper
pens

166. Sort it out
Preparation: write out words from a familiar verse onto slips of paper and hide them around the room.
The task is for the children to search around the room and find the slips of paper. When they have all been found, ask the children to put the words into the right order so that they form a verse which they are already familiar with or which they can learn.

> **tip**
> If a child begins to deviate from the task, or use the equipment in a laborious or exaggerated fashion then he is not focused on the activity. And if the child is not focused then the value of the activity is nil. Stop and do something different!

167. Partner balances
Arrange your players into pairs of similar heights. The pairs sit back to back on the floor with their elbows interlinked and push down with their feet until they are able to stand up. Alternatively, the pair can sit facing each other with their feet touching and holding hands. This time they pull each other to try to stand up. This will help them to work together.

168. Spirals
All players hold hands in a line. The leader walks the players around and then leads the line into a Swiss roll. Then the person in the centre of the spiral climbs over and under arms to lead the line out of the spiral.

you will need...
buckets and spades
a beach!

169. Sand sculpture
In groups, players can make an island out of sand and decorate it. Or they may choose to make characters from a story or even build a boat or rocket with seats and steering wheel! There is no end to what you can do with sand (see illustration)!

you will need...
scraps of fabric
needles
thread
PVA glue
glue spreaders
scraps of bric-a-brac
sequins
scissors
felt etc.

170. Collage work

Group members work in pairs to create a collage or painting taking part of a story as the theme, for example, 'Noah's ark'. Each pair then bring their work to the whole group and discuss the processes they have used to create that picture. The paintings are finally all put together to make a group masterpiece!

you will need...
an OHP
paper
pencils
scissors

171. Silhouettes

Using an OHP, project the shape of an object onto white paper on a wall and then draw around the outline to make a silhouette. Do this with several shapes. Then fill the shapes in by cutting and sticking collage materials, or by painting, to make a corporate collage.

you will need...
an assortment of Lego pieces

172. Lego land

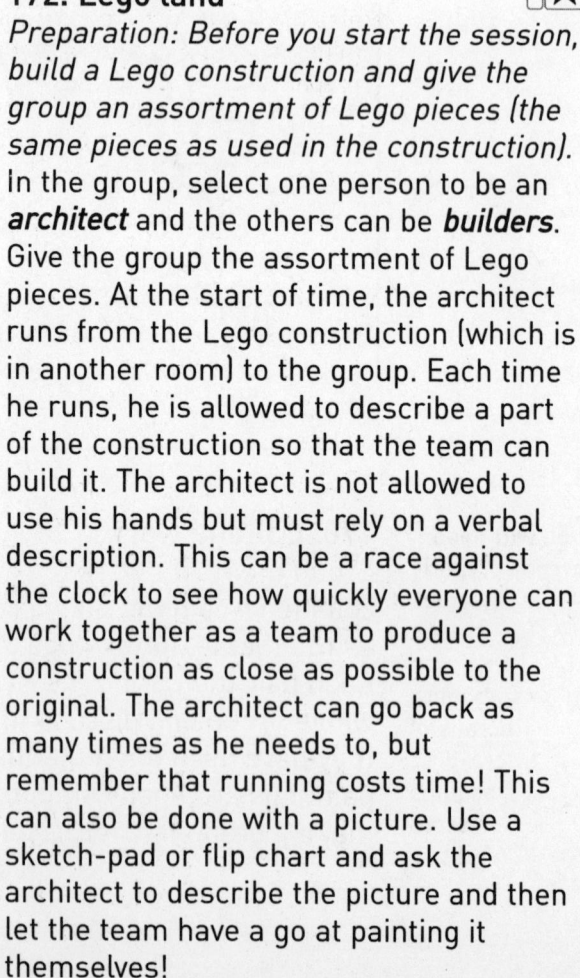

Preparation: Before you start the session, build a Lego construction and give the group an assortment of Lego pieces (the same pieces as used in the construction). In the group, select one person to be an **architect** and the others can be **builders**. Give the group the assortment of Lego pieces. At the start of time, the architect runs from the Lego construction (which is in another room) to the group. Each time he runs, he is allowed to describe a part of the construction so that the team can build it. The architect is not allowed to use his hands but must rely on a verbal description. This can be a race against the clock to see how quickly everyone can work together as a team to produce a construction as close as possible to the original. The architect can go back as many times as he needs to, but remember that running costs time! This can also be done with a picture. Use a sketch-pad or flip chart and ask the architect to describe the picture and then let the team have a go at painting it themselves!

> **tip**
> Some games are competitive but you can eliminate the competitive element to focus on the task.

> **tip**
> Always have extra activities up your sleeve in case your children lose attention. Running games are good time-fillers. You may also run out of activities and still have a few minutes to fill. Or, it might just rain! **Be prepared!**

you will need...
disposable cameras

173. Click photography
In teams, with a disposable camera per team, tell a story using a series of photographs. Or, take photos of unusual objects and, when developed, the others have to guess what they are, for example, the inside of an exhaust pipe.

174. What do you need? (discussion game)
The leader tells the group they can spend £100. What would they buy? As a team they need to decide what would be a good use of the money for the whole group.
The leader then tells them that they are refugees. They have no home, no food and water is scarce. Ask them to make a list of things they would buy if they had £100 to spend. What is the difference between what we need and what we want in life?

you will need...
a bench
blindfolds

175. Line up
Without being able to speak to each other, players have to line up along a bench according to different criteria; for example, in order of age (oldest on the right, youngest on the left); in order of height (tallest on the right, smallest on the left); or in order of birthday month (those with birthdays in January on the left, those with birthdays in December on the right). If you don't have a bench, you can play the game on the floor. Try blindfolding players, but this time you can let them talk!

you will need...
rope
torches
first aid kit
strong shoes and protective clothing

176. In the dark
Preparation: set up a trail by tying thick rope around trees.
In the summer, if you are fortunate enough to be able to go away with your group, try setting up a night trail. The idea is that the children follow a trail, without knowing where they are going. They must always hold on to a rope that will lead them in the right direction. This will build up their confidence in unknown situations, allow them to help each other, and have faith in the rope. The rope can be tied around trees and the trail may follow a path, lead through a stream and up and down hills. Leaders must always be reassuring and remember to carry a torch, just in case!

you will need...
hula-hoops

177. Hula-hoop game
Players stand in a long line and hold hands. Two helpers hold a hoop so that it is sideways on, and the whole group must get through the hoop without unlinking hands, as quickly as they can. You can time it and then see if they can beat their record.

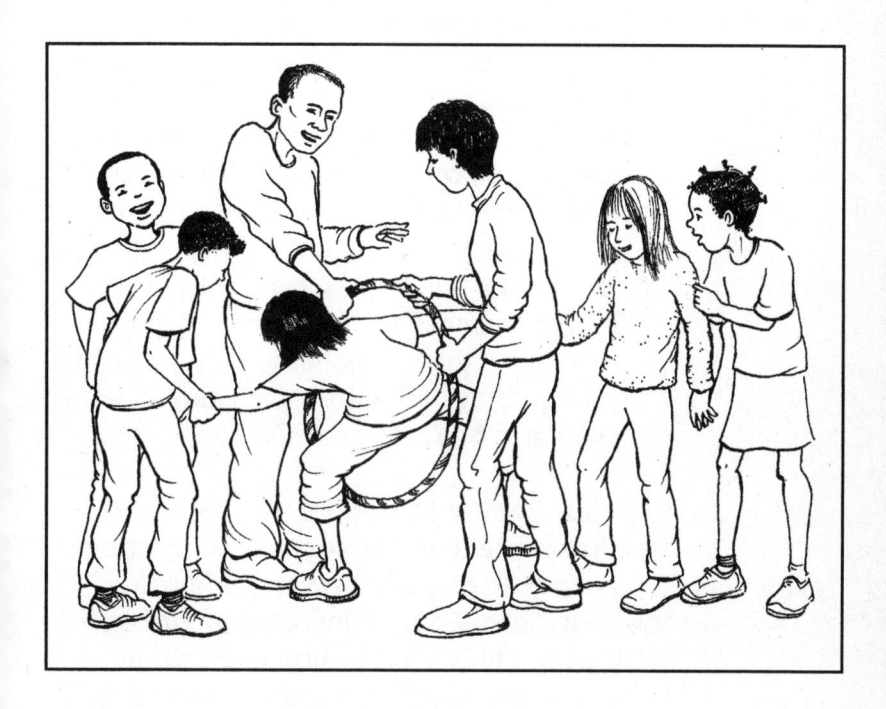

you will need...
several sheets of newspaper

178. Shrinking islands
Split the children up into four groups of four. Give each group a double sheet of newspaper which they must all stand on. No one in the team must have their feet on the floor. Once they have achieved this, fold the newspaper in half and ask them to stand on it again. Keep on repeating the folding and standing until the paper is

too small to be able to fold. They will have to devise a strategy for getting the whole team off the floor and on the paper! This game is good for breaking down physical barriers.

179. Waxworks
Arrange the players into groups of four and let them name themselves A, B, C and D. C is blindfolded and D leaves the room. Meanwhile, A moulds B into a statue-like shape or posture. Blindfolded C then has to feel B to discover his shape. A then brings D back into the room and C then attempts to recreate the shape on D. When the game is over, the blindfold is removed so that everyone can see how the new shape resembles the original one. If there is time, you can play this so that each player has a chance to be A, B, C and D.

180. People to people

you will need...
a CD player
CDs

Play some loud and fast music for the players to dance to. When the music stops, shout out an instruction for body parts to touch, for example, elbow to elbow, knee to knee, head to head etc. When you shout 'people to people', the whole group have to squeeze up to each other as closely as they can.

tip
Question the players quickly after your explanation of a new game to see if they have understood what you have said.

you will need...
several boxes of a variety of sizes and shapes
paint
newspaper
glue
scissors

181. Build a church!
On a Sunday school anniversary fun day, one group of people built a church out of boxes, paper and paint. It even had a steeple and was big enough to fit children inside. It took over an hour to make and people were involved for as long or as short a time as they wished, while other activities were going on. It was a collaborative activity involving most of the congregation.

you will need...
paper
pens
felt tips

182. Story board
Choose a favourite Bible story and break it down into scenes. Artistic ones in the group can draw pictures to form a story board. Others can write captions and speech bubbles, while others can colour or paint. Then you will have your own Bible story cartoon strip!

you will need...
paper
pens
felt tips

183. Newspaper reports
Choose a favourite Bible story to report in a newspaper. The group can be made up of journalists, writers, researchers, illustrators and editors. Nominate everyone to have a job and collaborate together so that you can present your report to the other groups.

184. Treasure trails

You can set a trail around your church or grounds by asking players to follow a series of clues and answer questions on the way. Try trails with co-operative tasks for the team to do, for example, a construction made from bodies; how many people can you fit into a telephone box? You could also give each group a camera in order to provide evidence of their tasks!

185. Three-legged games

Three-legged activities are great fun and initiate co-operation, as players will discover that they will find their task very difficult without it! Use skipping ropes or old tights to tie legs. *But don't tie too tight.*

a) Three-legged aerobics – tie the right leg of one player to the left leg of the other player. Then play music as in normal aerobics and get your players to do simple movements, for example, lifting arms and legs, star jumps and hops. They will discover that it is not as easy as it looks, and that they really need to concentrate to get it right!

b) Three-legged obstacle course – tie players' legs together, as above. Then ask them to tackle a simple obstacle course, for example, travelling over a bench, under a net and through a hoop. Make sure that there are no winners or losers in your game, and that everyone is congratulated for completing the course.

you will need...
cones
football

c) Three-legged football slalom

Using the cones, set out a simple slalom course (see figure). Tie legs together as described above. The task is for the pair to dribble the football around the slalom course with as much accuracy as possible. Each player can kick the ball, but the secret is to make little kicks so as to keep the ball under control. Speed is not essential here; again this is not a race. Congratulate all players when they complete the course.

you will need...
a double sheet
a plastic sheet
paints
felt-tip pens
paintbrushes
water pots

186. Banner making

Using a large sheet and poster paints, paint a banner. Designs can be drawn onto an acetate, projected onto the sheet, then traced on. All that the group needs to do is to paint in the design. This looks very effective and can be displayed in your church as a reminder of the activity time you have had together.

187. Being Bartimaeus: blindfold games

- Try doing an obstacle course while wearing a blindfold.
- Identify household objects or foods by feel, taste or smell while wearing a blindfold.
- Identify another child by feeling their hair and face while blindfolded.
- Fall back: a blindfolded person falls back into the arms of one player in a circle and is then passed around the circle by the others.
- Walk across a set of chairs, like stepping stones, while blindfolded. This may require a helper.

These activities are great for leading into Bible storytelling, or stimulating some sort of discussion, and can be done with all ages!

tip

Don't be put off because some games seem foolish or simple: the simplest games are often the most effective, easiest to follow, and most fun.

you will need...
a large sheet of paper
felt pens

188. Large wordsearch

Preparation: devise your own wordsearch.

The task is for the whole group to complete the wordsearch. It is fun to lay the wordsearch out on the floor and for everyone to ring the words they find with felt-tip pens. I have done a simple one for game 190: Food wordsearch, but the more words and the larger the grid you use, the better. You can theme your wordsearches on various topics, from Bible stories to current pop stars!

you will need...
pens
paper
tape recorder
Bibles
materials for creating sound effects

189. Radio plays

The task is for the group to produce a play based on a Bible story, which would be suitable for radio. First select a Bible story and read it thoroughly, in a variety of versions, if possible. Then choose how it may be written as a script. You may choose to use the 'Dramatic Bible' which has speech marked as in a script. Then select events that will need sound effects and choose household materials that you can use in order to create these effects. When you have written your play, you will need to rehearse before recording it. Good stories for radio plays are: Paul and Silas in prison (Acts 16:16–36); The Good Samaritan (Luke 10:25–37), and the battle of Jericho (Joshua 6).

tip

Did you know that we remember 30% of what we hear, 50% of what we see and 80% of what we do?

190. Food wordsearch

Find the following foods in the wordsearch below:

FISH AND CHIPS	LASAGNE	PIZZA
PEAS	RATATOUILLE	TOAST
CHEESE	ICE CREAM	SAUSAGES
SOUP	HADDOCK	SALAD
CUSTARD	POTATOES	YOGHURT
MEAT		

F	I	S	H	A	N	D	C	H	I	P	S	A
B	C	A	A	D	E	B	P	I	Z	Z	A	F
G	H	L	D	I	J	E	E	C	K	L	U	M
N	O	A	D	T	P	A	A	E	Q	R	S	S
T	U	D	O	R	V	N	S	C	W	X	A	I
D	P	Z	C	U	A	S	B	R	C	D	G	T
Q	R	W	K	H	E	C	H	E	E	S	E	T
L	A	S	A	G	N	E	R	A	T	Y	S	E
U	W	P	U	O	S	I	O	M	E	A	T	H
P	S	A	S	Y	D	F	G	H	G	J	O	G
K	L	D	R	A	T	S	U	C	G	M	A	A
N	O	P	O	T	A	T	O	E	S	P	S	P
R	A	T	A	T	O	U	I	L	L	E	T	S

you will need...
a magazine
scissors
paper
pens
glue

191. Human pyramid
The task is for the group to form a human pyramid, by forming four tiers of people, all kneeling. The bottom tier will have four players kneeling, the second tier will have three players on their backs and forming the next tier. The third tier will have two people and, finally, a single player will kneel on top. This will take good strategy planning and discussion, particularly in how to get players onto the pyramid.
NB I would recommend that you use crash mats for this activity or, if possible, a soft surface to land on.

you will need...
paper
pens
safety pins

192. How many words?
Preparation: write letters on squares of paper.
At random, give a square of paper to each of your players. They choose a letter and write it on the paper, which they then pin to their shirts. Split the players into evenly-sized groups. The task is for each group to form as many words as they can using the letters they have in their group. They needn't use all the letters at once, but must spell each word out, by standing next to each other. The people whose letters aren't being used turn around so that their letter doesn't show. How many can each group get? There is no winning team, as the draw of the letters is completely at random. But you may like to see if each team can do the game again and make more words the next time.

you will need...
a musician who is able to play the piano or guitar, and able to work out chords to a melody

193. Songwriting

I have used songwriting as a collaborative activity with many groups of children, and the outcome has always been one where the children have been very proud of their collective effort, and have grown closer as friends in the process. I have a method for songwriting, and have used this with children aged between 7 and 16 years old.

1. Think of a theme for your song.
2. Brainstorm ideas around the theme – use words and phrases. At this stage try not to contrive phrases into lyrics.
3. Using different colours of marker pen, circle the words and phrases that you think will be appropriate for a chorus, verse 1 and verse 2. You may even want to add a bridge section after a chorus, so select words for this too.
4. Start to put the words and phrases into a rhythm structure, to take the form of lyrics. Some sort of melody may come in at this point. As you put together the lyrics, think of ideas for a melody and try to work the two together. Repetition is good, particularly in the chorus section.
5. Work on the lyrics and melody together, and try out new ideas as you go. Keep evaluating what you have got. and make changes until a song is created.
6. The musician must then put chords to the melody, so that the group can sing it together.

Over the page is an example of a song written by children aged 11. The ideas came from them, with assistance from me. But the key fact is that the groups all gelled and worked together in songwriting and produced a great end product!

Children of the world

Chil-dren of the world come on__ and lis - ten:
try and keep the world in good__ con - di - tion.
You're not on your own so let's keep it that way__
save the world to - day!__ Save the world to -

-day! It's a super planet, you can't put a price on it. We have the power to create a better world. A bright future is all we need, because the world is in our hands.

themed activities

Theme nights or theme-related activities are great fun. They give an opportunity to dress up, to discover new things and to become somebody else for a while. They are great for family events too, as people of all ages can take part in the activities. It is also good to have some sort of theme-related food. That is always the fun part! Here are some suggestions for themes with related activities.

194. Australian night
- **Loud shorts** – your players can be encouraged to wear bright shorts and shades for your event, and you can take on names such as Bruce or Sheila, and say 'G'day' frequently in an Ozzie fashion!
- **Making hats** – use corks and string stuck around the perimeter of a hat to produce an Australian bush hat.
- Produce some examples of **Aboriginal art**. Look in library books or use posters you may be able to get hold of.
- **Decorate boomerangs** – make a template of a simple boomerang shape. Your group can draw round, cut out and

decorate the boomerang using paints, pastels, crayon, felt tips or any other media you have available.
- **Games** – try playing games with titles that can be adapted. For example, 'Duck and goose' can be adapted to 'Koala and crocodile' for the evening.
- **Please Mister Crocodile** – this game involves a chosen player to be Mister Crocodile, who stands with his back to the group. The group then chant, 'Please Mister Crocodile, can we cross the water?' Mister Crocodile then replies, for example: 'Only if you're wearing red.' The players wearing red then try to cross the room to get to the other side, but Mister Crocodile turns around and chases them. If a player is caught, he then becomes the next crocodile.
- **Didgeridoo** – as above, but decorate long cardboard tubes with aboriginal designs using pastels or chalks.
- **Sing-song** – how about singing 'Waltzing Matilda'?
- **Barbie on the beach** – a barbecue is a must for an Australian event. Hold it on a real beach if possible, but if not you can 'pretend' a beach!

195. Irish night
- **Irish dancing** – this is great fun. If you have someone in your team who is able to teach a few steps, that would be ideal. If not, watch a Riverdance video, and try to recreate some of the steps!

The fun is in everyone doing it wrong or badly. Everyone is in it together, so just have a go and enjoy it.
- **Fake Guinness** – pour cola into cups and place a scoop of ice cream on the top. The ice cream will froth and give the effect of a head on Guinness!
- **Irish boutique** – because green is the colour of Ireland, your group could all wear green clothes, paint their faces green and spray their hair green with wash-out coloured spray.
- **Relay races** – try running relay races, but done several ways, eg backwards, three-legged, blindfolded. Players can run backwards, dribble a ball and carry an egg and spoon.
- **Sing-song** – this is a good opportunity for a sing-song around the piano. Popular Irish songs are 'Marie's Wedding', Danny Boy', and 'Wild Rover'.
- **Shamrocks** – give cut-outs of shamrocks to the group and on each leaf of the shamrock they can write a prayer – a praise prayer, a sorry prayer, a thank-you prayer, a please prayer and two others of their own choice.

196. African event
- **Making masks** – look at examples of African art in library books. There are many elaborate designs and your group can design their own or copy one they like, using stiff card, coloured paper, scissors and glue.

- **Music making** – instruments can be made out of basic junk items. Also, if you have instruments you could make jungle sounds, or create a rainstorm or a dry desert land with sound.
- **Sing-song** – popular Christian songs can be sung in African languages, for example, 'We are marching in the light of God' can be translated into 'Siya hamba kucanyen quen cos'. 'God is so good' can be sung as 'Mungo nume (pronounced 'noo-may') moi, Mungo nume moi, Mungo nume moi, nume moi, quango'.
- **Fruit salad** – select a number of exotic fruits and, in the group, make a fruit salad. Be careful with sharp knives around small children, and consider general health and safety in the kitchen.
- **Face painting** – again look at pictures of some of the tribal native Africans and try to recreate them using face paints.
- **Sounds and pictures** – if you have a spare room available, have slides of scenes of the rainforest showing and music of the forest playing in the background. This can give people an opportunity to relax and take some time out from activities. Slides and CDs can be bought or borrowed from the library.

> **tip**
> In your theme nights, try to link your activities to the children's life experiences and ask what they have learnt, for example, a moral, a new type of behaviour or a link between different communities.

197. Highland games

- **Making kilts** – give your group lots of pieces of newspaper, Sellotape and string. It is their task to make a kilt which they will be able to wear for the duration of the evening.
- **Tossing the caber** – everyone can have a go at this. It is just a bit of fun; don't get too bogged down in distances and measuring results. Your caber can be a large plank of wood, which has been sanded and is safe to use, or a long cardboard tube. Use anything that is shaped like a caber and relatively heavy.
- **Haggis throw** – fill lots of small water bombs with water. The task is for players to throw the bomb (the 'haggis') to each other for as long as they can without it bursting.
- **'Highland fling'** – why not do some Scottish dancing? You can get records from the library to play and let everyone have a good knees-up!
- **Games** – organise events for the group to join in with as and when they please. For example, 'dwoil flonging' is a wet teatowel-flinging game. Each player dips a teatowel into a bucket of water so that it is wet, holds it by a corner and flings it as far they can! You can do other 'throwing' events such as welly throwing, jelly throwing, paper aeroplane throwing and 'javelin' throwing, using bamboo or balsa wood sticks. Just be careful that your

activities are well supervised and well spaced out to avoid accidents. And again, don't get involved in any result recording. Joining in should be the fun part.
- **Three-legged relays** are popular, as are any of the other games in the Running games or Messy games sections.
- **Food** – why not provide some haggis for your group, but make sure that there are plenty of alternatives, as not everyone will like it! You could also make **shortbread:** this is very easy to do and doesn't take long to cook. Look in any good cookbook for a recipe.

198. Space event
With thanks to Phil Brown for ideas from his holiday club materials.
- **costume making:**
  silver clothes: anything that looks remotely metallic will look totally at home in outer space. Use black bin liners with the bottom taken out for the outer garment and use foil, egg boxes, silver spray, card, etc to decorate.
  Space age shades: cut out a template of the shape of a pair of sunglasses. The group can decorate them in any way they wish, using foil, stars, sticky shapes, etc. Stick coloured cellophane over the eye holes, then punch a hole into either end of the shades and tie a length of elastic to them, so that the shades can be worn all night!

Moon boots: transform your footwear into something unrecognisable by adding foil shapes, and spray white laces with silver spray to thread into boots.
- **Face painting** – good toy shops will sell face paints with gold, silver and other metallic colours. Try making up your group into space-age men and women by painting their faces and spraying gold or silver spray into their hair. Make sure that the spray will come out in the wash!
- **Space food** – make shortbread biscuits, or simply buy a packet of biscuits, and decorate by covering with white icing and putting silver balls on the top. Confectionery balls can be bought in supermarkets.
- **Space construction** – give your group the task of designing and building a construction for the space age, using junk materials (for example, different-sized boxes, paper, sweet wrappers, egg boxes), foil, Sellotape, glue, silver spray, etc.
- **Games** – you can adapt many of the running games into games with a space theme. For example, game 141: Captain's on board can be adapted so that the commands are space-related. The children can run to parts of the room signified by parts of a rocket, and commands could be such as *'moonwalk'*, where they walk slowly as if they were on the moon; *'dodge the*

meteor!' where they bob down and cover their heads; '*Captain Picard's on board!*' when they can stand to attention (Captain Picard is a character in *Star Trek: The Next Generation*) and, finally, '*flying through space*', when they can run around the room with their arms above their heads and their hands together, to look like a rocket.

199. Caribbean event
- **Crafts – Treasure islands**: take a lump of clay and mould it into a mountain shape. Cover it with sand, and then use pipe cleaners, paper, sponge, plant oasis and papier mâché to make trees, houses and other landmarks for the island.
- **Treasure maps** – draw a treasure map on paper and colour in using crayons. Then dip the map into tea and leave to dry. The map will curl and look 'old'. Roll it up and tie a ribbon around it to finish.
- **Dancing sailor** – cut out the shapes of the head, arms, legs and body of the sailor. Attach the parts of the body together using split pins. Also attach string to his legs. When you pull the strings, his legs will move as if he is dancing!
- **Nautical mobile** – use coat hangers as the basis of your mobile. Draw and cut out shapes of nautical items, for example, a ring, an anchor and a ship and, using a needle and thread, attach the shapes to the coat hanger.

- **Tug of war** – this is competitive, but also facilitates group work. Take a long, thick piece of rope, and tie some cloth to its middle. Each team holds the rope at either side of the cloth. Each team pulls on the rope at the same time until the cloth goes over a centre line.
- **Sing-song** – sing 'Island in the sun', 'Yellow bird', and other Caribbean songs.
- **Drinks** – try serving some exotically-coloured cocktailes (non-alcoholic, of course). Provide simple recipes for three or four different cocktails and get young people to be the barmen. Key ingredients would include things like ginger beer, lemonade, fruit juices, cherryade, etc.

quizzes

Quizzes are great for a number of reasons. They are fun and children love them. They are a fantastic way of reinforcing your teaching, as when you ask them questions based on your teaching, your players are effectively retelling what they have learnt.
If you have a quiz every session, this gives them an incentive to listen! My quizzes are always based on sheer randomness. They normally involve a player answering a question, and that player doing a task with a completely random outcome, for example, taking a label off the quiz board to reveal a number or letter. Sometimes I split the children into teams and sometimes I make the whole group do a task against the clock, or a previous group best. In any case, I always say 'there is absolutely no skill involved in this quiz – it's all completely random!' If a child gets a question wrong, I then ask another child from that team, and keep on asking players in that team until the correct answer is given. But normally, the questions are so simple that the opportunity to get them wrong is very slim. I hate making a child feel that he has let his team down. The player who answers the question correctly can then have a go at the task. Note: always write your questions in advance, have plenty available, and keep the quiz fast-moving.

Here are a selection of quiz formats that have worked for me, with questions based on a variety of Bible stories. The quizzes are based mainly on the same format, and you may like to experiment with this and devise your own ideas.

200. Clock quiz

you will need...
card
scissors
a marker pen
split pins

Preparation: using card, cut out two circles and mark round in five-minute intervals, as on a real clock. Also cut out 'hands', and attach one to each clock by sticking a split pin though each hand and a circle in the centre of the clock. Cut out smaller circles, the same number as there are questions. Write numbers onto the circles: 5, 10, 15 and 20. Put these into a bag. Prepare your quiz questions. Ask teams one question at a time. When a player answers correctly, he then closes his eyes and pulls out a circle randomly from the bag. The number on the circle will designate how many minutes the hand on the clock goes round. The winning team is the one that gets round the furthest. You could also try it as a timed activity, to see how quickly the whole group can get around the clock, from 12 o'clock back to 12 o'clock.

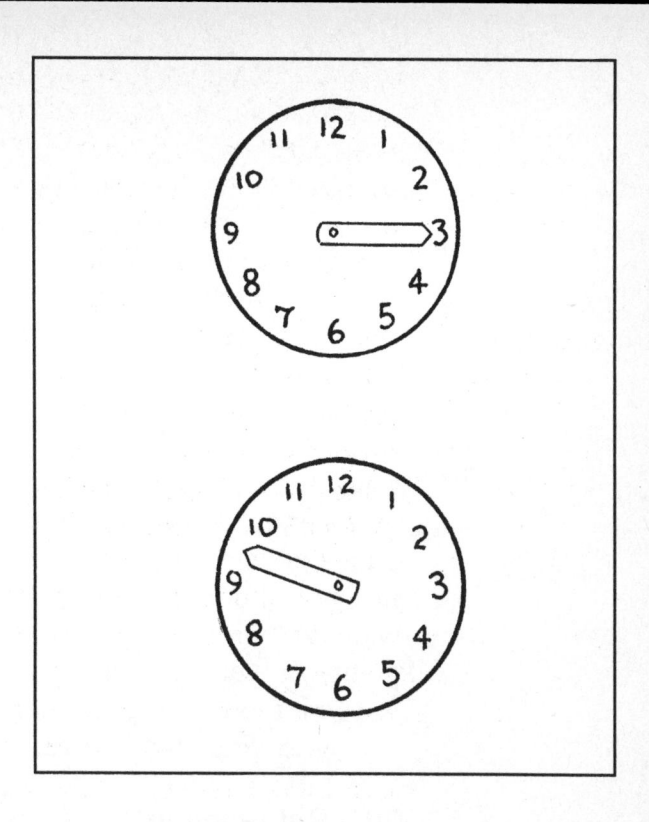

you will need...
cards
paints
scissors
silver foil
a dice
a flip chart or
board

201. Party time
Preparation: Cut out two large circles of card for plates and, using the silver foil mounted onto card, cut out the shapes of two knives, two forks and two spoons. Then draw, paint and cut out the shapes of party food, for example, cake, crisps, burgers, cheese on cocktail sticks, biscuits and sandwiches. Do two of each, then make up a 'price list'. So, for example your sandwiches will be 6 points,

a burger 5 points, biscuits 3 points, and so on. Stick the shapes of party food onto the board and mount the plates and cutlery onto larger card or a board. Prepare your quiz questions and you are now ready to play.

Ask the team(s) one question at a time. When a player answers correctly, he then rolls the dice. The number on the dice will designate which piece of party food is to be placed on the team plate, and how many points the team has now got. The game ends when the food has all been allocated to plates, and then the total number of points is determined. The winning team is the team with the most points. Or you can play against the clock to see if the whole group can attain or beat a previous high score.

you will need...
card
paints
marker pens
scissors
Blu-tack

202. Ruthaphone

Preparation: Take your mobile phone and copy its shape onto large and stiff card. Draw all its features, and give it a name. I call mine 'Ruthaphone' and have the text written as if it was the network name. Then cut out key shapes identical to the ones you have drawn on the phone. Cut these out and draw identical icons onto them. On the reverse of each 'key', write a comment that relates to a phone; for example, engaged, call waiting, call minder, no answer. Also, on a few of the cards, draw the symbol of two phones making a connection. Stick these cards over the keys on the card phone using Blu-tack.

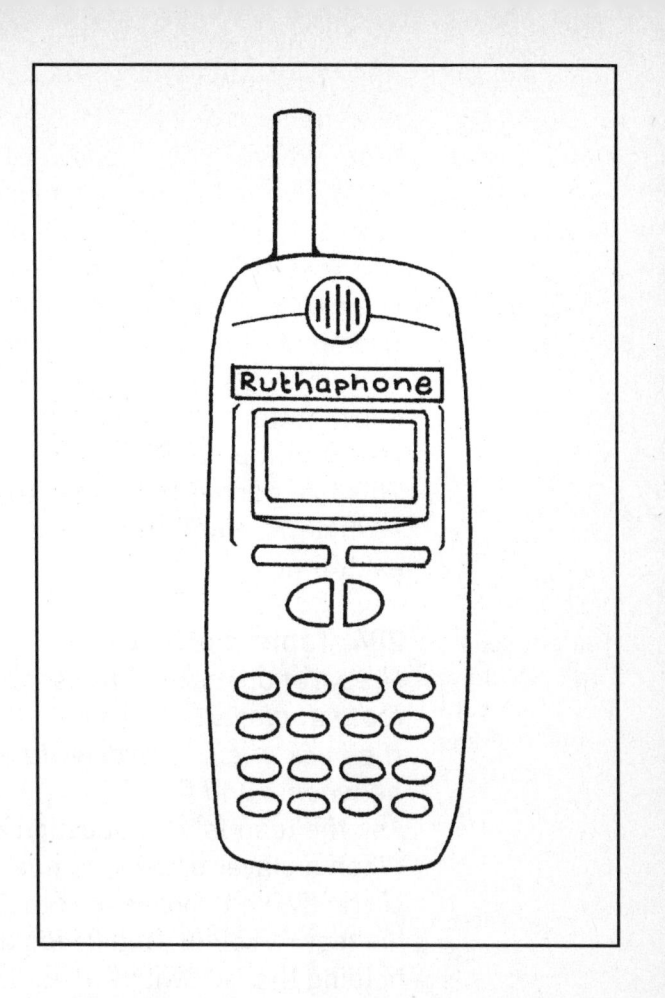

Ask the team(s) one question at a time. When a player answers correctly, he then chooses a key on the phone and removes it, revealing the comment on the reverse. When a mobile-to-mobile connection has been found, the team has won a point. The winning team has the most points.

you will need...
plastic cups

203. Tall tower

Ask the team (or teams) one question at a time. When a player answers a question correctly, he takes a plastic cup and places it on top of another plastic cup, bottom touching bottom. The next player to answer correctly then places another cup on the tower, top touching top. As more players answer questions, they add cups, bottom touching bottom and top touching top, until the tower falls over. This is a good quiz to do with the group as a whole, seeing how tall the tower can get each time.

you will need...
two colours of card
marker pens
scissors

204. Table football

Preparation: cut out the shapes of table football players in two colours of card. On the back of each card, write a number between 1 and 9

Ask the team(s) one question at a time. When a player answers a question correctly, he chooses a football player of his team's colour, and keeps the card, holding the side with the number on it close to his chest. At the end of the quiz, tell each team to arrange themselves into any order, in a line, each player still concealing his number. When they have done this, ask them to turn their football players over to reveal their digit, and therefore the whole team reveal a large number. The team with the largest number is the winner. This game is completely random and quite a good laugh when the winning team has scored 658923 points!

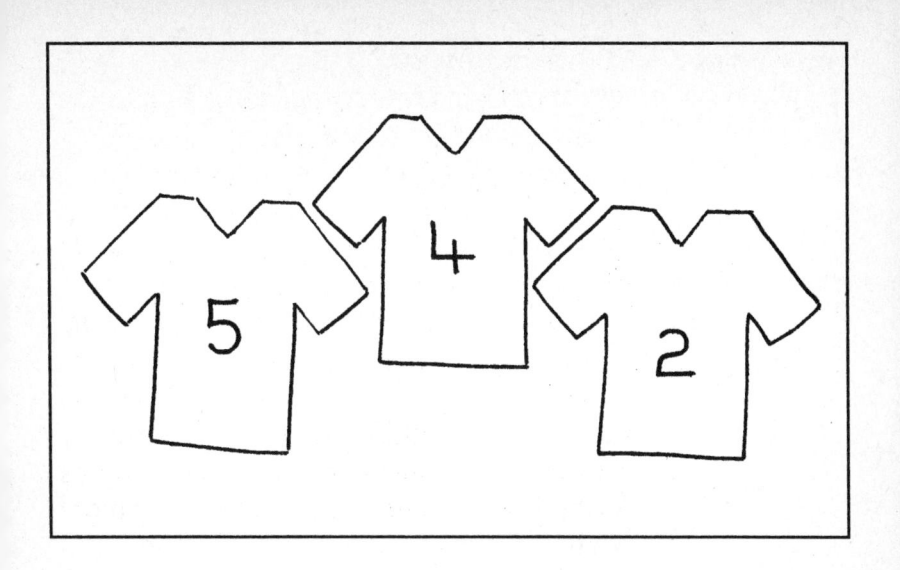

205. Last man standing

Preparation: prepare quiz questions with multiple-choice answers.

All players stand. Ask the first question and give the possible answers. The players vote for their answer by standing on one leg if they think the answer is A, putting their fingers in their ears if they think the answer is B, and putting their hands on their heads if they think the answer is C. Read out the correct answer. The players who voted for this answer stay standing while the others sit down. Play this until you have one player left standing at the end, or until the whole group is out. It is fun to ask impossible questions about yourself or your team in this game, to which they will have to guess the answer (this makes the game completely random, but great fun)!

you will need...
four pieces of A1 card
paints
marker pens
scissors
Blu-tack and pencils

206. Gone fishing

Preparation: Draw two grids, each 3×3 squares, on two of the pieces of card. In three of the squares on each grid, draw some fish. On the other two pieces of card, draw a picture or logo. Then mark out an identical grid on these with pencil and cut the card up so that you have nine squares for each grid. Stick these squares onto the original grids, so that the logo is formed. Each team has one grid.

Ask the team(s) questions, one at a time. When a player answers correctly, he peels off a square of card to reveal either a fish or a blank square. The winning team is the team to have the most fish when all the questions have been asked.

title index

1–10. 33
Absence of sound   71
Adverts   53
AEIOU   44
African event   141
All change   77
All the fish in the sea   104
Alphabetti spaghetti   61
Amoebas   109
An arty problem   118
Apple bobbing   63
Are you listening?   36
Australian night   139
Baked beans   100
Ball circle   26
Ball madness   25
Balloon bash   115
Balloon shave   66
Banner making   130
Bear in the cage   34
Being Bartimaeus   130
Bubbles   105
Bible stories with a difference   54
Billy Beater   72
Birthday cake   116
Birthday present   87
Blind square   117
Blob   51
Body language   47
Bottle pick up   112
Bridge building   110
Budge   99
Build a church   127
Call out   20
Captain's on board   105
Caribbean event   146
Cat and mouse   102
Cat and mouse   90
Celebrity crocodile letters   35
Celebrity mix 'n' match   18
Chain tig   97
Chance music   72
Character empathy   58
Chart music quiz   10
Children of the world (music)   136

Chinese actions   45
Chocolate quiz   13
Click photography   123
Climb the mountain   88
Clock quiz   150
Collage work   121
Contrasts   74
Cookie jar   35
Co-op letters   108
Cornflake crazy   64
Crocodile letters   35
Crossing the poisoned river   113
Dodgeball   23
Duck and goose   99
Eclair memory verse   62
Electric fence   113
Escaping noise   43
Eye contact   46
First impressions   15
Flash cards   72
Food wordsearch   132
Football quiz   11
Foot painting   64
Footy fan   14
Fred quiz   12
Fruit salad   32
Gone fishing   156
Group juggling   26
Group rondo   73
Gunge tank   67
Hand ball   29
Hand band   71
Hidden shoes   89
Hidden treasure   89
Hide the beater   73
Highland games   143
Horsemen, knights and cavaliers   51
How many words?   133
Hula-hoop game   125
Human pyramid   133
I am not guilty   44
Ice melt   47
Identikit   9
"If you love me honey, smile"   50
Instant drama   53

In the dark   124
In the hole   87
Introductions   21
In yer face!   19
Irish night   140
Jammy noses   66
Jelly walk   66
Jump in   50
Keys of the kingdom   108
Knees pile up   39
Knotty problem   110
Lap ball   28
Large wordsearch   131
Last man standing   155
Lego land   122
Line up   124
Log roll   108
Machine   53
Magic gobstopper   43
Magic microphone   34
Making waves   87
Messy morning   62
Mexican wave   87
Mexican name wave   19
Mirrors   48
Modern storytelling   54
Mouse tails   106
Mushroom   85
Musical hoops   117
Musical jigsaws   118
Musical laps   32
Musical Mexican wave   73
Music man   38
Newspaper reports   127
Nintendo touch   98
Obwisanna   74
One man and his dog   107
Parachute Bible stories   91
Parachute prayers   91
Parachute volleyball   90
Partner balances   120
Party time   151
People to people   126
Photo story   49
Picture postcard   48
Ping-pong crazy   111
Play a picture   79
Popcorn   98
Press conference   57
Props   33
Queenie   28
Radio plays   131
Rainstorm   78
Rats and rabbits   102
Ring on a string   31
Ruthaphone   153
Sad and happy faces   80
Sand sculpture   120
Say what you mean!   50

Sea storm   88
Sharks   88
Shoe swap shop   33
Shrinking islands   125
Silhouettes   122
Skin the snake   109
Songwriting   134
Sort it out   119
Sound collage   71
Sound dominoes   76
Sound effects   81
Sound picture   44
Space event   144
Spaghetti quiz   61
Spiders web   112
Spiders web talk time   116
Spirals   120
Story board   127
Story time   103
Stuck in the mud\Snowmen   99
Table football   154
Tadpole   24
Tallest tower   110
Tall Tower   154
Tent   91
The animal game   38
The bear and the honey pot   37
The flour game   64
There's a hole in my bucket   65
The wall game   52
Three-legged games   128
Traffic lights   101
Train spotting   31
Treasure trails   128
True\False   20
Turtle   88
TV report   57
Under the sea   86
Up and under   86
Vocal games   42
Warm up   41
Water bombs   65
Water challenge   34
Water tower   67
Waxworks   126
Weather forecast   78
What are you doing?   18
What do you need?   123
What's my line?   45
Where do you live?   12
Which country?   18
Which town?   17
Who are you?   11
Who is it?   115
Who's counting?   14
Wordkit   10
Writing wall   119
Your number's up   97

Other games resources from Scripture Union

Theme Games
Lesley Pinchbeck

Games are fun but they can be more than that - they can be experiences through which people learn, grasp concepts and take ideas on board. When working with young people, games can be an integral part of a whole learning programme.

With around 150 games for 9-13 year olds, arranged thematically and well-indexed, you should always be able to find just the right game to link with the rest of your programme.

0 86201 841 2
£5.99

Coming soon!

More Theme Games

Over 100 brand new theme games for use with your group!
Available July 2002

Over 300 Games for all occasions
Compiled by Patrick Goodland

A revised edition of this popular handbook including outdoor games for groups, parachute games, sports day ideas, indoor games, party games and games for travelling.

1 85999 264 1
£6.99

Absolutely Everything: Through the Bible in 11 game-based sessions for 11s–14s

Terry Clutterham

An incredibly creative resource taking you from Genesis to Revelation, helping you and your young people to:

- see the Bible as one big story.
- wonder at God.
- understand why Jesus came.
- want to be and remain on God's side in this big story.
- trace the themes of 'creation', 'promise', 'revelation', 'judgement' and 'salvation' in the Bible and in your own lives.

1 85999 432 6
£7.00

You can obtain any of these books from:

- Your local Christian bookshop
- Scripture Union Mail Order: Phone our Subscriptions and Mail Order Department on 01908 856006.
- Online: Log on to www.scriptureunion.org.uk/publishing to order securely from our online bookshop.

Prices are correct at time of going to print.